Poetry Ireland Review 119

Eagarthóir / Editor

VONA GROARKE

© Poetry Ireland Ltd 2016

Poetry Ireland Ltd/Éigse Éireann Teo gratefully acknowledges the assistance of The Arts Council/An Chomhairle Ealaíon and The Arts Council of Northern Ireland.

Poetry Ireland invites individuals and commercial organizations to become Friends of Poetry Ireland. For more details, please contact:

Poetry Ireland Friends Scheme, Poetry Ireland, 11 Parnell Square East, Dublin 1, Ireland

or telephone +353 1 6789815; e-mail info@poetryireland.ie

FRIENDS:
Joan and Joe McBreen, Desmond Windle, Neville Keery,
Noel and Anne Monahan, Ruth Webster, Maurice Earls,
Mary Shine Thompson, Seán Coyle, Henry and Deirdre Comerford,
Thomas Dillon Redshaw

ISBN: 1-902121-62-7
ISSN: 0332-2998

ASSISTANT EDITORS: **Paul Lenehan** and **Sally Rooney,** with the assistance of
Daniel Tatlow-Devally and **Orla Higgins**

IRISH-LANGUAGE EDITOR: **Liam Carson**

DESIGN: **Alistair Keady (www.hexhibit.com)**

COVER CREDIT: from 'Arashiyama', by Hugh O'Conor (**www.hughoconor.com**)

Contents PoETRY IRELAND REVIEW 119

Editorial

"Come we to the summer, to the summer we will come", John Clare declared in 'To Summer'. (That the poem swivels full-turn into its concluding lines: "I hunger at my meat and I daily fade away / Like the hedge rose that is broken in the heat of the day" need not worry us overmuch: we already know there is a price to pay for these few heady months, and we pay it, bulked up with additional interest, for a long seven months and maybe eight. But right now, we have no care for money: we have enough for 99s tucked into our shoes, and tonight, we will catch mackerel off the rocks and fry them up in the last of daylight, and we won't need dosh for that.) Though we may well be nudging towards its outside edge, (more after-sun than suncream; more crumbs than picnic; more sand in the beachbag than beachbag on sand), we still bask, we do, in the season when, according to William Blake, "we lack not songs, nor instruments of joy" ('To Summer').

Come winter, we'll watch shadows bloom on the wall, count daylight on one hand, and measure rainfall in fathoms. But now is high hours and, if they slip a little every day, we can try not to notice and try harder not to care. Now is the aftermath of summer but, just about, summer still: sand between our toes and pale bands on our arms and fingers when we take off watches and rings. Two months ago was giddy summer; now we may settle for languid summer and dog days, or we may imagine gathering berries fervently and stockpiling them in freezer drawers to see us through dark days.

Now is not October, in shoes that cover all the foot, and the timer on the heating lurching backwards, day by day. Now is yet for taking photographs and not for putting them in albums set to close in on themselves in seldom-opened drawers. Still, the sea sings preppy songs and forgets all its dirges and hymns. And if it's no longer quite the five a.m. start or relished 'daylight in the shutter' of Seamus Heaney's 'High Summer', there's still a deal more of the bright-faced, feckless new friend about it than the spurned companion with a pet rat and a way with irony to whom we will apologise for our absence, sourly, next month.

So why can't we be happier in our summer poems, why can't we just enjoy it? The first line of John Keats's "Written on a Summer Evening" loses no time in reminding us that, 'The church bells toll a melancholy round'. It's not encouraging.

But Philip Larkin, with his famously sunny disposition, perhaps he can cheer things up? The title of 'Mother, Summer, I' sounds promising. While stanza 1 recalls his mother's preference for well, anything but summer, stanza 2 opens hopefully (especially if we overlook the 'though'):

> And I her son, though summer-born
> And summer-loving, none the less
> Am easier when the leaves are gone …

No, that's no help, he has surrendered, thrown in the (beach) towel. Perhaps, we could turn to America, bask a little in their higher temperature? Here's Jane Kenyon, 'Coming Home at Twilight in Late Summer':

> And then we noticed the pear tree,
> the limbs so heavy with fruit
> they nearly touched the ground.
> We went out to the meadow; our steps
> made black holes in the grass;
> and we each took a pear,
> and ate, and were grateful.

And suddenly, we're in the meadow, where we want to be. And though there may be black holes in the grass, nothing can bruise that redemptive pear; the simple, beautiful fact of it that cannot be gainsaid.

And then, with summer on our hands and in our mouths, we head to ee cummings' beach, to lose and find ourselves.

> maggie and milly and molly and may
> went down to the beach (to play one day)
>
> and maggie discovered a shell that sang
> so sweetly she couldn't remember her troubles, and
>
> milly befriended a stranded star
> whose rays five languid fingers were;
>
> and molly was chased by a horrible thing
> which raced sideways while blowing bubbles: and
>
> may came home with a smooth round stone
> as small as a world and as large as alone.
>
> For whatever we lose (like a you or a me)
> it's always ourselves we find in the sea

It's a poem that runs through shallow rockpools of narrative and imagery, keeping up with itself, just about. And when it finds itself alone, it looks up at the high, blue sky and is timid. And for comfort, it picks up a satiny phrase – sea-washed and shiny words that will soon dull to grey, almost certainly, but haven't, not just yet.

The year turns. The calendar flips over a new month, and the year must recalibrate. And so must we. Here at Poetry Ireland, we find

ourselves not in the sea, but on the comparatively dry high ground of
11 Parnell Square East, our new home. Over the coming years, we plan
on a major restoration of this beautiful building which will be, in time, a
permanent, redoubtable home to Irish poetry. The summer may well be
on the wane, but our future is, quite wonderfully, on the up.

This being Ireland, let us finish with rain; firstly, catalogued by
Geoffrey Hill, (who died on 30 June), whose 'Old Poet With Distant
Admirers' extends to us, minutely: 'dark-blistered foxgloves, wet berries /
Glinting from shadow, small ferns and stones'. And then by Yves Bonnefoy
(who died on 1 July), whose 'Summer Rain' redeems the world (the trans-
lation is Paul Weinfield's):

> And when we gathered
> sticks and fallen leaves,
> the smoke and then
> suddenly the firelight
> were gold again
> in that golden night.

Emma Neale

WILD PEREGRINATIONS

From the lookout point
of sleep's edge
the years spread back
with all the pinprick fires and dark clutches
of an old, uneasy settlement.

The thoughts watch themselves
the way one falcon acts silent sentinel
to another across the blue whisper
of desolate distances.

Then as if it believes
its moon-washed, grass-gold skin
will be ample camouflage –
the dart, the jink,
the erratic dash and back-dash:
hope's wild peregrinations,
love's blood-sweet liqueur
crammed beneath its skin.

Ryan Vine

BONFIRE

Three snowflakes for every black chip of soot
we send into the sky. And he can feel the snow always

falling, my father, who orders me to ready the fire.
So I pile chopped buckthorn at the edge of the yard

where the switchgrass hasn't yet turned to swamp
and drizzle from the Folgers can dirty oil

across the branches. The bark on the grey kindling
peels and darkens where the fuel soaks in,

and beneath the heap – and for the fuck of it on top –
I crumple open sheets of last week's *News Tribune*.

The forest is flashing its bonewood, but under my jacket
I shine like a marathoner, like a sword in its sheath.

When father comes stumbling through the snow with a drink,
I pack the pipe, pass it, pack it again. Every time

I take a hit I hear the stylus drop and drag
through the groove: I'm not afraid. I light the fire.

I'm happy with what happens a hundred years from now:
the soot I loose gathers like a new moon. My son,

his son, staring through the snow-dappled sky, both
swear they can see it, spinning in perpetual eclipse,

even though – like me – they know they lie.

Ryan Vine

WORK

According to the song coming from their car,
these four dudes don't give a fuck.

The doja – strong as a flattened skunk –
smells delicious, and I bob my head

instinctively as they pass. I remember
it's not as simple as just not giving a fuck.

I know now that the hip-hopper was trying
to write: *I'm scared and I'm lonely and I can't*

believe what the people I love most do
to each other. I want to carve a wet hole

into the skull of my beloved
and stare into it until I see my face.

I'm pushing a stroller the size of a wheelchair.
My two year old's munching on browned

apple slices, from which I carefully removed
the skins this morning so he could hold one

in each hand and easily bite from both.
It's not true about trouble, about time:

I haven't healed. I'm trying to forgive
myself without the help of a god.

Sarah Byrne

GIN

I'm under the quilt when you insist
on extolling the spirit's provenance:
the flourish of bog myrtle and star anise,
the murmur of rowanberry and angelica root.
You tell me it must be the quinine that's
making me queasy and the metronome
I hear tapping is the prophylactic popping
of the fuchsia. And even though I have sown
myself into the bole of a tree, I will wake
naked to an oaken jacket seething on the floor.
There will be rings of lichen curling around
my tongue and decades of juniper beads
stuttering their rosary in my ear.

Sean O'Brien

THE PRIVILEGE OF PRIVACY

John McAuliffe, *The Way In* (The Gallery Press, 2015), €11.95.
Caitríona O'Reilly, *Geis* (Bloodaxe Books, 2015), £9.95.

There have been times in recent decades when the great indoors looked
almost like forbidden territory, a zone ringed by signs warning of anti-
personnel mines. If domesticity had a place in poetry, it seemed as if it
should have overtones of something else: threat, atavism, the end of civi-
lization. But of course those proceedings have to start somewhere. Peter
Porter once satirised the work of his friend George MacBeth, who had
made a sinister ritual out of boiling a lobster on the stove, while his own
'The Sadness of the Creatures' found 'two people not disposed to argue'
suddenly overwhelmed by a sense of futility and desperation reaching
far beyond the confines of a London flat. Ciaran Carson's 'Dresden' sent
and received shockwaves from the flattening of the city by the Allied air
forces in 1945. Is it possible to write about domestic happiness, or something that promises it, or the modest hope of it?

For John McAuliffe seems to think so. At the centre of his excellent fourth
collection, *The Way In*, home is to be found. It visits the mind when the
speaker is absent from it; it shapes his activity; it is where he is coming
from or going to; and in some subtle way it renders all other activity
unofficial, displaced by claims the poet shows no sign of resenting. A
meeting in the street with a friend in 'Stand-off on Santiago Street' is a
rush of anecdote and observation enjoyed under the pressure to resume
the school run. It ends with poignant farce, when a man screams 'I fuckin
love ye Louise' from the car he then fails to drive away from the sight of
a man and woman talking. The outdoors, it seems, may be what befalls
those who are unfaithful to the lares and penates and lose their grip on
the mysterious privilege of privacy.

For McAuliffe, our own privacy is a mystery kept from us by the day-
to-day of children, things needing fixing, routines, holidays, changes of
season in the back garden and the 'happy storms' of marriage. It is both a
great gift and one beyond possessing – and its intense, durable necessity
is only emphasised by an encounter with someone whose home has been
breached by mortality. In the tenderly observed 'The Coach House' an
elderly woman, partly disabled and suddenly widowed, is trying to main-
tain the garden which is 'the least of her problems'. By contrast, the effort
to get on with work in 'The Retreat' (we may suspect that the speaker
has not gone anywhere but that everyone else is temporarily away)
involves a comic nightmare of distraction from the task in hand, for

example by flies, until 'I swat them, not with the paper but the Bloodaxe Neruda, / *splat*. Or a sound very like that. And that.'

The central sequence 'Home, Again' expands the frame of reference to take in some of what Derek Mahon referred to as 'what is meant by home' in the historical context of war, colonization, decay, migration and return. It sounds like a set-piece, but it reads as a set of very attentive improvisations to which McAuliffe's prosodic flexibility is well attuned. He begins with a discussion in a pub with friends, though poetry takes some time to surface after one of them announces he intends to return to Ireland. This is, in some not entirely clear way, connected with his sense that poetry has become a career rather than a vocation, and that the death of Seamus Heaney marks a point beyond which the public life of the art may enter a final decline. Why this should prompt a return to the equally careerist Republic is neither explained nor, perhaps, amenable to explanation, having to do with the instincts that inform the rest of the sequence and are subject to its scrutiny. 'And take this away', McAuliffe writes, 'I'm not taking it anywhere else. It isn't / a state of the nation, or of / "contemporary mores". It's trying to be straight, / ish'. We are, it seems, where we find ourselves, on the road or in what turns out to be home, making something out of it, neither masters nor servants of what we may not choose to call destiny.

Geis is a welcome return from Caitríona O'Reilly. Her third collection takes its title from 'a supernatural taboo or injunction on behaviour', and the book operates in terrain where experience and imagination often take on the contours of myth. We might see this as a way for the poet to discern order in experience, but much of the time the sense of myth and ritual does not stand in for the everyday so much as displace it. *Geis* is not a book of explanations, though O'Reilly's wide learning and infectious curiosity are often apparent.

'The Winter Suicides' considers those to whom 'the world gives ... a stone', and who were 'least kind' to themselves. The play on 'kind' carries us into a paradoxical sphere where scientific facts are treated as if they should offer mythical or religious completeness and consolation (which they don't) but / and where despair is itself a myth-driven response to experience. 'Like us, they were unable to believe / / the frequencies of light concerned them; / they followed the logic of the particle down / / to the sea floor, literalists who sought a solution.' The restrained elegance of O'Reilly's expression here, and the way she finds a place for wit without dispelling the gravity of the theme, seem more effective in evoking the tragedy of the suicides than many louder utterances. She is, of course, entering a discreet plea for seriousness, whereby an interest in the nature of knowledge is an urgent human necessity. Elsewhere, in 'Comparative Mythography', she observes that with the displacement of the explanatory structures of mythology by science,

> Each day brings less, now,
> to believe. Knowledge means

> not that it is true, but that it works:
> the elimination of air in a jar
> makes smoke trickle downwards

The facts seem not to answer to human needs which are experienced as real, not as pre-scientific illusions. O'Reilly concludes 'The Winter Suicides': 'In the silence, in the immeasurable interval / / between systole and dawn, we ask: / she gives us the snowdrop's sidereal pallor', and the snowdrop with its head 'heavy as lead' in Ted Hughes's words, is linked to the remotest constellations, while we ache to fill the space between.

In 'Blue Poles', art itself (the paintings of Jackson Pollock) is depicted as a means of keeping open the possibility of meaning which the world itself may seem to have foreclosed:

> The West was won and there was nowhere left to go
> so you vanished into a dream of perpetual motion
>   knowing that once to touch the surface
> was to break the spell, but that while the colours hung
>   on the air an instant, there was no such thing
> as the pushy midwife, the veiled mother in the photograph,
>   the rich woman's bleated blandishments.

A second, phallocentric myth – of toxic femininity in various guises – enters the poem to suggest that the escape into art is first formed and later determined by the very constraints the work opposes or seeks to ignore. It's not, of course, a new idea, but O'Reilly shows it as continuous with Pollock's revelatory work, so that we are not diverted into the biographical reductiveness so commonplace in the discussion of art of all kinds.

Although she writes a good deal about people, one thing O'Reilly isn't much concerned with is 'personality'. 'The Servant Question' narrates the life of a Catholic housemaid – used, blamed, discarded – alongside a quotation about servants from Virginia Woolf. The latter reminds us of what Woolf, for all her enlightenment as 'a literary woman', actually was in terms of class assumptions and presumptions. At the close, O'Reilly records that what she records:

> are not my memories,
> yet they move in me continually

with a river's moment,
breaking and reforming its ripples, its patterns,
through all my rooms and days,
my work all about me.

The simultaneous lucidity and complexity of these lines, with their
balance of contradictions, their ostensible calm and their sense of the
extending shadow of a myth inside which we live, underline the fact that
O'Reilly is an outstanding poet in her generation.

Evan Costigan

WINTER PICNIC

Whenever my father returned from his travels, the house filled with tales
of moaning bears and night skies fractured by the branches of trees
he'd rolled his bed under. Jade and camel-bone snuff bottles
bullied rock fragments to the precipice of our mantelpiece.

There were mornings we woke to new alphabets on bedroom walls
or the bugled blast of a *sankha* last sounded on monastery grounds,
where he'd persuaded a monk to barter it for a penknife. He spoke
of the ruby-red eye of a hare in the Arctic, sudden blizzards,

spheres of perfect silence, a beast abominable only
in its loneliness. Within weeks, he grew quiet, until the tug
of the next adventure. We were bolder in his absence.
That day we emerged from the brambly tundra of the lower garden,

arms and faces scissored by briars, to burst into the attic. I flung open
the battered suitcase with broken clasps. Inside were letters
tied with twine, sellotaped maps, out-of-shape matchboxes
that rattled with the husks of winged insects. We found a journal.

Opened, it released a withered stem for a bookmark. There were faint
sketches of flowers, a bird with a Mohawk of feathers. On a loose page,
the portrait of a woman with a hook nose, her eyes pencil-grey tones.
An entry: *Fatherhood?*

That last trip. His face shaggy as a yak when he got back; how he
hugged each one of us and then hung on. An excursion our mother
forbade we ask about; from our listening post on the stairs, we learned of
a dust storm so fierce he thought the world was coming undone.

After he remained, we had lessons in languages, our dreams swelled
with seas of moving grasses, snake charmers, the call to prayer.
Most of all, I remember that picnic. The five of us on a blanket,
drinking tea from small glasses under trees stripped of leaves.

Majella Cullinane

WINTER SOLSTICE

> The day dawns, with scent of must and rain,
> Of opened soil, dark trees, dry bedroom air.
> Under the fading lamp, half dressed – my brain
> Idling on some compulsive fantasy ...
> — Thomas Kinsella

In the dark I cannot say what the day begins with. The curtains are closed
and dreams still drowse beneath our blankets. There's the routine
of ablutions, and feeding, of dressing and leaving to get through, before
I can walk Back Beach and breathe the scent of stillness and frost in the air,
pass the young man searching for his future on the tip toe of his shoes,
who neither sees me nor the road ahead. But who am I to say
as I trot down the hill and around the corner, find it there as it is each time
as if I were expecting it to be parcelled up and delivered
  elsewhere in the night.
Does it take longer for a place to disappear than a person?

There, in the cluster of boat houses, the floating skiffs, the scene
a friend told me once was too perfect, that would be ripe for a murder.
Rather the ghosts of fishermen leaving the small wharf
rowing out to sea, marvelling how the sky changes each day,
how this morning clouds are thickets of orange and mauve echoed
  in the waters
folding beneath their keels, welcoming the curve of each man's offering.
Later the women will rinse the dishes, scrub children's faces,
watch them skip up the gravel road, past Iona Church, to the schoolhouse
where just yesterday I noticed a line of clothes circling in the afternoon wind.

I too find myself in a bedroom now, the reflection of myself in the window,
only the line of my torso, my arms in a white woollen jumper.
Below me the neighbour's house; behind that a tree stripped by winter.
I am neither idle nor riveted by my eyes, but at this moment
the letters race to catch each other across the space; the sound
in my ears is piano keys and the slow stretch of bows against strings.
It is the day before the shortest day of the year. The sky is grey,
  it has started to rain.

David McLoghlin

BLUE DARK

I think I have seen it repeated: someone
silhouetted, as if climbing a line,
rising slowly. When he broaches the surface
he starts to die – his colours gasping
on the scumming pan of the concrete
some crowded day at the beach. There is
always that ocean. All I give him is the swarm
and bloom of algae in The Narrows:
not enough oxygen. There is another sea
when I go into the thicket
of an hour without guilt or kinship,
to be able to come back like someone
walking out of water. Albatrosses rise
to 10,000 feet, cock their wings, and glide
until the sound of spray wakes them.
When I am there, silence can open
like a sea rose, billowing. He goes down the ladder
of blue-dark, coming to rest on the substrate
where there is another kind of breathing.

Gwyneth Lewis

PERSEPHONE

                    'Look at me, Ma!'
                    Walking the beam,
                    She wobbles then
                    Pirouettes
                    En pointe
                    On a proton.

Daughters never see danger,
Which is their charm,
Till they come to harm:
Flowers scattered in the bubble chamber.

Then, implacable mother, I
Search under winter's gravity waves,
Find where she hides.
Pomegranate seeds
Pulse in her gullet,
A fact, irreducible. Her eyes:
Dilated to mirrors of black
In which I loom large.

In light again
On visits home
She dances at double strength.
The pinprick pupils
Have shut me out.

Gwyneth Lewis

NEST
for Susan

A home fell from the sky. I picked it up.
It said: 'Obey

The law of taking this and that
(a whisp, one tuft
of hair, five stems) from anywhere.
Arrange your scraps,

The boldest first. The trick's
Not too much craft: the whole
Must not amount to much,

Or seem to.' Like
A coracle! A cup! A cap?
Should I put it back?

'Don't fuss. I'm logos now,
Just loose enough. Here,
You have me. Yes. I
Insist.'

Seán Lysaght

ARCADIA AND ITS ENEMIES

The Irish Poet and the Natural World: An Anthology of Verse in English from the Tudors to the Romantics, edited by Andrew Carpenter and Lucy Collins (Cork University Press, 2014), €39.

This remarkable anthology is the latest instalment in a project that began in 1998 with the publication of Andrew Carpenter's *Verse in English from Eighteenth-Century Ireland*, to be followed six years later by his *Verse in English from Tudor and Stuart Ireland*. Like its predecessors, *The Irish Poet and the Natural World* does more than underline individual reputations, it also sets out ley-lines for literary tradition in Ireland. The ambition of this multi-volume presentation is clear: to articulate a vision of Irish poetry in English from the Tudor period onwards, and establish a cultural continuity based on language, in defiance of the fractures and disturbances of history. This anglicisation of Irish literary tradition is apparent if we compare any of these anthologies with Douglas Hyde's *Literary History of Ireland* of 1899, which deals almost exclusively with Gaelic literature.

This new volume is unlike its predecessors in that it does not simply rest on historical periods, but also takes a particular thematic view, by selecting poetry with reference to landscape and the natural world. There is a theoretical and academic drive behind this focus, which informs the extensive introduction by Andrew Carpenter's co-editor Lucy Collins.

In their search for poems that qualify under the 'nature and environment' rubric, the editors have assembled a wide body of work, some of it occasional (the death of pets, the surprises of weather, etc.) or oddly miscellaneous. Early accounts of hunting and angling provide a rich vein for the editors, before nature gets sentimentalised in the eighteenth century. Swift's 'A Description of a City Shower' and his poem on the Carbery Rocks on the coast of West Cork are both included here, showing how a writer of strictly urban and classical taste can be recruited. There are examples from the Tudor period onwards of arcadian, picturesque and romantic visions of the environment that amount to a substantial legacy: they even comprise an alternative strand within Irish experience, amounting to what Robert Macfarlane has referred to as an *utinam*, an 'if only' history. We get scarcely a whisper here of the Celtic and Gaelic legacy of nature poetry, which the cut-off date of 1820 strategically keeps in check, ahead of the explosion of translation and rehabilitation of that legacy in English from the mid-nineteenth century onwards.

In a characteristically witty aside, John Banville has said that nature was something invented in the eighteenth century. While this holds true as a dismissal of nature in its benign, romantic aspect, founded in the enlightenment, it doesn't measure up to the rich traditions of representation of the natural world from the early modern period onwards. Writers such as Spenser and Milton may have been unsettled by the chaos of wilderness, but their imaginations roamed at will across alternative landscapes from the classical tradition. These bountiful settings derived in large measure from Virgil's pastoral and georgic writings and their arcadian idyll.

Spenser's fragment from the Mutabilitie Cantos of *The Faerie Queene* is a familiar early example of the classical imagination at work in a disturbed colony. Before contemporary troubles, in an Irish Golden Age, the goddess Diana and her companions ranged across a rich Munster landscape 'Of woods and forrests, which therein abound, / Sprinkled with wholsom waters'. Spenser uses a variant of the Actaeon story to write an allegory explaining how this exquisite setting, with its nymphs and satyrs, was cursed by the goddess and reduced to ruin,

> Since which, those Woods, and all that goodly Chase,
> Doth to this day with Wolves and Thieves abound:
> Which too-too true that lands in-dwellers since have found.

Spenser's myth-making is of great interest because he sets the arcadian idyll so dramatically, and knowingly, against the backdrop of a disturbed country.

From the seventeenth century onwards, the pentameter and rhyming couplet were used so extensively in narrative and descriptive poetry that it took special powers of style or subject matter to add variety to the effect. (This virtual monopoly would only be broken when the influence of Wordsworth's blank verse began to be felt after 1800). In a few instances, it was Irish weather that added excitement to the monotony of this format, as in Payne Fisher's 1645 account of a boatload of Civil War troops being wracked by storm and sea sickness on Lough Neagh, or George Wilkins' description of a day's hunting being brought to a close by a thunderstorm.

In the following century, there is a close correlation between an Ascendancy order of estates, parklands and demesnes, and the poetry of Georgian celebration; one excellent example of this neo-classical taste is the extract from Thomas Parnell's 1713 eclogue to Health, which Alexander Pope praised as one of 'the most beautiful things I have ever read'.

> Joy to my Soul! I feel the *Goddess* nigh,
> The Face of Nature cheers as well as I;
> O'er the flat Green refreshing Breezes run,
> The smiling Dazies blow beneath the Sun,

> The Brooks run purling down with silver Waves,
> The planted Lanes rejoice with dancing Leaves,
> The chirping Birds from all the Compass rove
> To tempt the tuneful Echoes of the Grove ...

Pope's admiration for Parnell was such that he edited his poems for publication after Parnell's early death in 1718.

Within this Georgian order, we can trace the emergence of a romantic fascination with the picturesque and the sublime from a very early date. James Ward's delightful hymn to the Phoenix Park (1718), delivered in the shadow of the Royal Hospital, includes this description of the river:

> Deep in the Vale old *Liffy* rolls his Tides,
> Romantick Prospects crown his rev'rend Sides;
> Now thro' wild Grotts, and pendant Woods he strays,
> And ravish'd at the Sight, his Course delays,
> Silent and calm – now with impetuous Shock
> Pours his swift Torrent down the steepy Rock;
> The tumbling Waters thro' airy Channels flow,
> And loudly roaring, smoak, and foam below.

As the picturesque tradition develops in the eighteenth century, we get an increasing sense of direct contact with the landscapes being celebrated by the poets. Samuel Shepherd's 1741 poem in praise of Leixlip is the first to engage the viewer as someone moving through the countryside, giving detailed descriptions of scenery and wildlife, so that there's a strong sense of natural objects breaking through the heavy layering of the literary apparatus. The same feeling, of direct engagement, emerges in William Balfour Madden's 1761 piece on Belle Isle Castle Estate on Lough Erne in Co Fermanagh. After a classical encomium to the big house and its setting, a party sets out on an angling trip, with the embarkation described in heroic, almost Homeric tropes:

> To Boat's the Word, to Boat, to Boat they cry;
> The Waters, Woods and echoing Hills reply.
> Rouz'd at the chearful Summons, one and all,
> At once we issue from the sounding Hall.
> Adown the sloping verdant Lawn we run;
> Full in our Sight descends the glowing Sun;
> The glad Attendants pour obsequious round;
> Oars, Nets and ready Tackle spread the Ground.
> A sumptuous Pinnace, near the Beach reclin'd,
> Spreads her bright Pennants to the curling Wind.
> Eager to quit the Firmness of the Land,
> Each Hero takes a Goddess by the Hand.

While poems like these create a Georgian idyll in an Irish setting, there are other landscape poems where political tensions disturb the genteel veneer. Goldsmith's account of the decline of the countryside in 'The Deserted Village' is matched in this anthology by angrier criticisms of the abuses of landlordism and accounts of rural poverty. In this vein, the anonymous 1781 poem addressed to the incoming Lord Lieutenant, the Earl of Carlisle, is particularly impressive, because it combines praise for the natural riches of Ireland with an analysis of economic subjugation and a Burkean call for religious toleration. Another, later poem of this kind, attributed to Anna Liddiard, is much more detailed in its account of the Carlow and Kilkenny countryside and combines romantic praise of scenery with georgic details of the farming year. There are many vivid touches throughout this extensive and important regional portrait, such as these lines on the sudden appearance of a whirlwind and the superstitious response of the peasantry:

> Amid the calm behold the whirling blast
> Rush through the grove, in wild disorder cast;
> Skim o'er the mead, and in its eddying sway,
> Sweep to the clouds aloft the new-mown hay:
> Or from the road the rifted surface bear,
> In circling column dancing through the air.
> The swains observe, with superstitious fear,
> And cross themselves, believing fairies near!

Towards the end of the period covered by this anthology, the work of William Hamilton Drummond has a special authority. His 'Hibernia' of 1797, just before the turmoil that would lead to the Act of Union, begins with an almost bardic address to his native country:

> Much injur'd Erin! Faction troubl'd isle!
> No more the land where Peace and Concord smile!
> Rous'd by thy wrongs to patriotic ire,
> For thee I tune the bold adventurous lyre ...

Then comes a dramatic passage where the island is called into existence by a Nature divinity. At 'her omnific word', Ireland's rocks and landscape are created; the classical Nature goddess

> With scenes Arcadian made thy landscapes teem,
> And realize each old romantic dream.

The account of Ireland turns on a familiar question: if Nature created such a benign place, why is the land so troubled by poverty and division?

The extract from 'Hibernia' concludes with a wish that Ireland be united with Great Britain, a reminder that patriotism finds many political expressions.

Drummond's vision of Ireland is informed by knowledge drawn from the Enlightenment and scientific tradition. In the second extract here, from his famous poem on the Giant's Causeway, Drummond shows that he can handle modern science alongside poetry of a classical pitch. In this, he is an exemplar of Enlightenment tradition. The most sublime passage of all shows the poet, accompanied by the figure of Science, flying through the cosmos like an angel in Milton, with all the old threats of ignorance and fear melting away:

> Where'er she turns, to earth, or heaven, she sees
> The real heralds of divine decrees.
> Now plunging downward, see her urge her flight
> Through the dark realms of chaos and of night;
> Now mid the zones, she spreads her wings afar,
> Soars to the sun, and visits every star,
> And scanning Nature's universal laws,
> Mounts from the second to th'eternal cause.
> Here, by overhanging rocks, where Danger keeps
> His dreary watch-tower trembling o'er the deeps,
> Th'adventurous muse's anxious thoughts explore
> What power of Nature formed the pillared shore.

There is no better example of how poetry, and the aesthetic, can embrace knowledge.

Work of this kind can often escape common recognition because of the ways in which secular knowledge and poetry parted company during the romantic period. The division was powerfully reinforced by Yeats's anti-secular mission later in the century, and his characterisation of Ireland as a pre-modern folk culture. Even earlier, Tom Moore salvaged his bardic instrument from the ruins of political defeat following the Act of Union. His particular strain of nostalgia in the *Irish Melodies* (1808) includes many references to the natural world that surely would have qualified him for inclusion here, were it not for the fact that Moore intro-duces an entirely new political note, keyed to the native tradition. And yet Moore is the Irish romantic poet par excellence, whose Irish lyrics reflect the political reality of post-Union Ireland and who was also fully at ease in the salons of Regency England. His omission from this anthology points to a possible sequel: a second volume of Irish poetry of the natural world, from the Romantics to the present day, beginning with Moore. In fact, the summary title of the present volume, *The Irish Poet and the Natural*

World, begs for a sequel to complete the record up to the present and admit the great riches of what Yeats called 'The Celtic Element in Literature', as he wrote, in 1898: 'Once every people in the world believed that trees were divine, and could take a human or grotesque shape and dance among the shadows of the woods; and deer, and ravens and foxes, and wolves and bears, and clouds and pools, almost all things under the sun and moon, and the sun and moon, not less divine and changeable …'

Seán Hewitt

SIRENS

Past midnight, the bracken scratches
its thin wrists. The sun too is restless
this far north; always a pink wick of light.

By the path, a circle of wild lupins hold
their upright spears, waiting for news.
I can imagine how they toll their blue bells,

hailing, luminous, and I bend to them,
listening at their hundred open mouths
so that for a while I fall under their spell,

sense my body swaying as if the waters
are being lifted in my ear. And so,
for a while only, I let myself stand

as one of these heavy flowers, collecting
the dark on my tongue; breathing in
and out; being moved, moving.

Seán Hewitt

CONNEMARA

> I will encounter darkness as a bride
> And hug it in mine arms.
> *– Measure for Measure*

All distance emptied, the world reduced
to an arm's length. The closeness of the night
is absolute: nothing to steady an eye on,
nowhere to rest a thought. My life is narrowed
to the ground beneath my feet. There is a guilt to it,
a clandestine hush to the fumbling of breath.
Whole fields have surrendered – the night
lifts its hood over them, calms them, sings a hymn
of warm silence to lull the grass to sleep.
A small wind brushes past my leg,
somewhere a bird settles in a hedgerow
or rests its full breast in the stubble of the corn.
The dark wants my life for itself. It raises its lips
to mine, its breath is in my breath, and I think
its face pauses before mine. Imagine its contours –
the deeper pools of blackness – its full embrace.
My limbs are buoyed helplessly by it, and I float.
I almost speak, but it stops me, lifts a finger
to the empty word of my mouth, and leans in.

Seán Hewitt

HARVEST SPIDER

how it sits at the centre of its legs, the knee-joints
raised over the globe of the body, how it can stand
in many places, making a bridge of itself, lighter
sometimes than wind, lighter than leaf, sending
each foot stepping in circular movements, how
its small seed of body must be suspended, held
lightly and assuredly, its life a glass of water
that must be carried home each day unspilt.

Frank Ormsby

THE CASH RAILWAY

The annual bus trip to Enniskillen
to buy a school blazer
ends in Ferguson's, Gents Outfitter,
with the little cable car of cash
they call the Cash Railway
whirring up the wire
to the office on the first floor,
its companion descending
at the exact same speed.
At the point where the two cross
there is nothing in the world
that is off-balance or out of sync.
You want to loiter there
for the next hour
and shout 'Bravo'
at every round
of funicular perfection.
But your mother is at the door,
lopsided with shopping,
reminding you that she has only two hands.

Frank Ormsby

OMAGH

'You'll land me in Omagh,'
my mother groans,
at her wit's end.
Omagh is where the birdies are.
The out-of-mind drift
out of sight a while,
then back among us.
It is said that madness
runs in families.
We mooch around our gate
and think of it travelling at speed
in the shape of Miss Carty,
who, home again,
has joined the Dippers
and cycles the main road
in suspenders and knickers.

Edward O'Dwyer

AUSTRALIA

At that point came the first signs
of tears on their way, and all
there was for her to do was to stand up
and to turn away

from the rabble of other voices,
all the clanking and rattling coming from the kitchen,
the ding of the till drawer closing,

face out the window of the café,
look through the couldn't-be-bothered weather,
through the lunchtime crowds,

zig-zagging
once, and again, and again, gaining the water's edge,
passing through lush Dutch fields,
past their waving windmills,

around Azerbaijani oil rigs,
through the syrupy air pollutions of Indian cities

and then out over more water, to another land's edge,
an exotic stretch of beach, her boyfriend there,
his hair grown longer, wavier,
a lighter shade now, one not unlike the sand,

the sun beating down
as he applies a generous squirt of sun cream
to the bronzed back and shoulders
of a girl that went to her school,

that she never got on with,
with whom, though nothing really happened,
there was a tension she couldn't quite put a finger on.

Afric McGlinchey

WHAT'S THE STORY?

John F Deane, *Semibreve* (Carcanet Press, 2015), £9.99.
Nell Regan, *One Still Thing* (Enitharmon Press, 2015), £9.99.
Martina Evans, *Burnfort, Las Vegas* (Anvil Press, 2014), £8.95.

The poets reviewed here reflect a triangular set of Irish poetic impulses: lyricism, wit and the *seanchaí* flair for storytelling. The common ground is how their poetry explores the past, both personal and cultural / historical.

John F Deane has long been a force in the Irish poetry landscape – founder of Poetry Ireland and this journal, a member of Aosdána, winner of prestigious awards, a prolific essayist, fiction writer and much-translated poet. He was a seminarian for a time, and immersion in the Latinate language has left its mark. In this musically cohesive collection, he dwells on the philosophical, spiritual, and religious issues inherent in grieving, feeling lost, or fearful: 'What do you say to the dying, when already / they have waded out beyond hearing', he writes in 'Driftwood', a poignant key poem that establishes the tone, grace and lyricism of a collection that is, essentially, an extended elegy for his brother.

The tone is reflective, though at times cut with an acerbic self-consciousness: 'grief thickens with its selfishness' ('High Tide'); 'I am standing, old and self-absorbed as Lear' ('Rain Falling in the Far West'). Idyllic childhood moments are recalled. In the poignantly titled 'The Living-Room', he incorporates both piano practice and the notion of outdoor escape in a single image:

> On the parlour floor, remember?
> just there, before the hearth, the river-otter pelt, sleek
> golden fur through the underhair, silk-feel and death-grin,
> how it brought into the room the stealth of water-dog,
>
> high-jinks and romping, teeth sunk in trout-flesh,
> secrecy of den and holt, the chill, the sliming ...We
> held to the basics, arpeggios, chords and scales;
> you mastered them, remember? They have eluded me.

There is a nod to Heaney: 'I will forge out words, plunge deep into language' ('Museum of Country Life'). This comfort lifts him from melancholia, reminds him that he is alive. Like Hopkins in 'Carrion Comfort', Deane chooses to 'wish day come, not choose not to be'. Instead of staring too hard at the brutal certainty of death, the speaker celebrates the sustaining force of poetry: 'the spirit holding // through the slow counterpoint and the unravelling' ('Theme and Variations').

Nell Regan's *One Still Thing* is a collection of emotional complexity. Her lyrics are sound-dominant, even where they are dissonant: 'Every // note, whoop and noise rattles' ('A composer walks the catacombs ...'). As with Deane's collection, it's a pleasure to hear the fluid music of vowels and consonants:

> Horizon tricks the eye, a sea –
> long gone – is sighted. A fossil
> lightly shifts, remembers tide.
> > – 'Santa Fe'

This habit of looking both into the far distance and microscopically, of shifting viewpoint, is characteristic. In 'Printers' Type', a young apprentice imprints his girlfriend's rear with the ink he cannot wash from his hands. 'The oncologist too // will guess his job by what / the x-ray will reveal. But that // is years away.'

Objects recur, taking on a talismanic power: glass, pearls, shells, gold. 'Imprint' is another recurring word in Regan's word-box, along with 'impress' and 'retort'. (I expected to read 'report' as the word follows 'sniper' and suggests a gun going off). These elements keep the collection cohesive through leaps in time and geography.

The use of conceit is another favourite device. In 'Feeding the Birds' she uses the story of St Kevin to teach mindfulness: 'How to focus, solely, / on the task to hand.' The task is the thing, as Deane also knows. 'Archaeology Class' brings to mind Frost's 'Mending Wall':

> *It's all words*, says one, as we reassemble
> with language of cist and corbel, each part
> of the dry wall back unto the cairn.

'Passage', a sequence of epistolary poems addressed by a famine emigrant to her sister, begins with a sea-passage. Like Martina Evans, Regan is adept at portraying character. Like John F Deane, she favours patterning and repetition. From the speaker's initial fearfulness at being abandoned ('Under my feet / the ground gives way'), she quickly reveals her essential strength and pragmatism – 'I am resolved' – and even a rebelliousness. She goes on a date with a 'half-Indian', even though 'I reckon doors will be / shut against us if we do take up'. (Later in the sequence, a child asks: *Tell us again uncle – how you scalped that squaw*'). Some poems are written in the voice of her lost betrothed, and here the language becomes filled with tools, the practical clatter of industry, as in Adam White's *Accurate Measurements*.

After being immersed in a previous century, it's quite a jolt to return to the present, although travelling by plane for the return journey, as a symbol, is effective: 'I see why they say / the psyche or spirit can't travel at this speed / that it lags behind at a walking or sailing / / pace' ('Jet Lag').

While autobiographical material will inevitably emerge, a seasoned poet becomes more interested in writing about what we learn, what we know, what we've been told, and what we make of this knowledge. In this third collection, Nell Regan has captured a resonant moment in history and allowed the stories of unknown individuals to flow around her own, creating an emotional connection across time and space. The recurring bridge is a perfect metaphor for a beautifully distilled collection.

Martina Evans, a multi-award-winning author of ten collections of prose and poetry, was hooked by the power of books from an early age. As the Graham Greene epigraph that opens *Burnfort, Las Vegas* tells us: 'in childhood, all books are books of divination'. This collection is an intimate portrayal of a family home, feisty mother and docile, evasive father who escapes, for solace, to his cats. Not just a personal retrospective divining, these distinctive poems weave in early influences, product names and era-defining cultural references.

The title poem reveals Evans' mastery of the apparently effortless anecdote, digressions that snap back to reveal an orchestrated circuitry, like a kaleidoscope. The poem begins with an Elvis shrine, opens to the pub, the street, out to where the 'mountainy men' live, then back to the pub and the shrine. In the interim, the place has transformed into Las Vegas, by way of New York. The conversational tone also establishes the voice:

> A few months ago
> the novelty mug frightened us all
> by spontaneously bursting
> into *Viva Las Vegas* and I took that
> as a sign, did what any
> Catholic would do – put up a shrine.

Like Regan, Evans has an eye to America, the richest source of cultural influence for a child of the Sixties – not just Elvis but Frank O'Hara and films like *My Darling Clementine*, which stirs up romantic associations with her own father ...

> I think of the story of Daddy suddenly angry
> one night he had enough
> and refused to be pacified with a drink
> which he sent flying down

the Formica like Doc
with the back of his hand

... although her father is really ...

more like Mack standing behind the bar
when Fonda asks, *Have you ever been in love?*
The small deferential bald head answers
subversively
No, I've been bartender all my life.

The Formica table reappears several times. In the prose poem, 'Daddy and Mae West': '*Come up and see me some time*, you said, patting the yellow Formica with swollen crooked hands, the morning Mae died and Mammy said there was more to you than met the eye'. Strangers sit there too: 'A thin nicotine man / legs crossed showing grey socks / sits at the end of the yellow / Formica table' ('Save Us'). The table becomes a symbol for the layering of family history.

Evans, like Paul Durcan, encapsulates her characters through gesture, physical feature or expression: a guard's 'pan loaf-sized foot poised / on the pedal of his Honda 50' ('Known to the Guards'); a doctor's breath, 'so wine-rich every morning' ('Substitute'). There is a poignancy too: 'ten children trapped / in a mushroom cloud of jealousy / over love spread too thin' ('Save Us'). It leaps clear of sentimentality, however: 'People have this idea of ghosts but isn't there a reason for everything? The howling? Sure, that was only the old dog, gone demented on her bed, turning round and round on top of the sheets and of course, they had to shoot him too, after' ('Ghost Story').

Like her influences, Joyce and Flann O'Brien, she is so naturally close to the spoken word, the rhythms and assonance are almost subliminal. But they are there. In fact, so much is layered here, the richness is palpable.

Marianne Burton

FILM NOIR

Le Jour Se Lève. La Grande Illusion.
Pépé le Moko. Quai des Brumes.

We watched them all last night in a great glut
with wine from Monoprix and reblochon and bread
and a flautist in the Rue Fleurus practising runs
until I began to link his thin downracing riffs
with Gabin dreaming of ships he never boards.

And now this morning's norming of the dark.
Cold air cleanses the sheets of last night's passion
and love seems less star-kissed more Silenus
from the Luxembourg Gardens, fat, drunk, falling off his ass.

One must be grateful dusk comes round so often.
Last night's lines can echo through the streets again.
Embrasse-moi encore. We have so little time.

Caitlin Newby

'HER SISTER'S WORDS INCITE THE BURIED FLAMES'

After Virgil's Aeneid *Book IV, ll. 54-89*

     Her sister's words incite the buried flames
of love, giving her hope, freeing her from shame.
Together they approach the temples of each god,
praying in turn for divine approval, offering
the choicest lambs for slaughter at the altars of Ceres,
Phoebus Apollo, and Lyaeus – and to Juno above all,
protectress of marriage bonds.
                     Dido, herself handsome,
pours seasoned wine out of a handsome golden cup
between the horns of a white heifer. Before the blood-
stained altars, in the sight of the gods, she paces,
taking up the day's offerings, gazing into the still-
beating chest of cattle, consulting their entrails.
Oh! not even poets know what promised words
might aid or mitigate the violent passion of a lover.
Entirely consumed, she says nothing of the wound
beneath her breast.
                 Dido wanders through her city,
wild like a wide-eyed doe struck by the steel-
tipped arrow of a passing hunter; he leaves her
running from glen to shadowed grove, the arrow fixed
into her bloody flank.
               She leads Aeneas through the city,
showing him her new Sidon, under construction.
She tries to speak, but can't. She craves to see day
turn itself to night, to hold another feast and hear
Aeneas recount, not for the second time, the siege
on Ilium, hanging once more onto his every word.
When everyone has left, when the moon has passed
through night and the stars urge sleep, she falls
crying onto the couch where Aeneas once sat.
She hears him when he's not there; she holds Ascanius,
the image of his father, tight on her lap, a trick
to satisfy this horrible desire.
              All work stops.
Towers stand half-built; boys no longer practice
war games; men no longer labour in the harbour
or along the city walls to make them impenetrable;
cranes stand still, their heavy loads suspended in the air.

Grace Wilentz

THE IGUANA DREAMS OF ITS MOM

Lazy I slept through the lunar eclipse and dreamt of my mother.
She has visited me only twice – in some mid-western supermarket,
       and again, in the stall of a Bangkok street merchant.
Each time the feeling was fuller than a phantom limb, for I think I
  have my heart
       back
before the backward fall of waking, where the strings of grief catch
  me and make me
       move.
I have lived through two eclipses – saw one on a beach with my
  mother, missed one
       in a dream with her too.

Tracey O'Rourke

THE THANATICIAN'S TRICKS

There is no sleep here – the duvet is hot
and malevolent; these heaped-up sheets

a counterpoint to the restless toss
of pine and lanyards.

My neighbour swears through the walls
her vibrator has let her down again –

its hum abruptly gone.
I hear the creak across her room

she's hunting for batteries,
I want to offer her this cigarette

but know she will refuse.
So I smoke it, slowly, alone.

I am breathed by memories
moon-handled this night

recalling how, when the freshly dead's eyes
will not close, the smallest corner

of paper towel beneath the lid
will do the job.

We cannot sleep like this.

Colin Graham

KNOWING AND LAMENTING

Paul Muldoon, *One Thousand Things Worth Knowing* (Faber and Faber, 2015), £14.99.
Paul Durcan, *The Days of Surprise* (Harvill Secker, 2015), £12.

'Think of how there lurks / in almost all of us a weakness for the allegorical.' In 'Dromedaries and Dung Beetles', from *One Thousand Things Worth Knowing*, Paul Muldoon tempts us to anchor his shifting, sliding allusive poetry. Allegory would suffice, for a moment, as a way of reading Muldoon. Things suddenly align and seem to be about to match up and make sense. Rhymes approach fullness, and the shape of a sonnet becomes clear. But then the poetry returns, via syncopated syntax and layered reference, to opacity, the very thing which tempts our weakness for allegory, and Muldoonian non-equilibrium is restored.

We know, now, how to read Muldoon, allowing his method its licence and his wit to play its way to a conclusion. *One Thousand Things Worth Knowing* is joyously Muldoonian. The quip about our weakness for allegory is not just Muldoon teasing his readers, but Muldoon reflecting on himself, and perhaps pointing to how we can see shapes, patterns and meanings lurking in these poems. *One Thousand Things Worth Knowing* seems less carefully structured than other Muldoon volumes (its occasional poems and the gathering here of some of the poems previously published in *Songs and Sonnets* explain this), but it does have recurrent obsessions which tempt allegories. The American Civil War and the Spanish-American War, for example, reappear across the poems, most centrally in 'A Civil War Suite'. Mathew Brady (the Irish resonances of his name are not allowed to slip away) was 'a dab / hand at fixing that *guerre* in Daguerreotype', and Brady starts off a poem which entwines Ireland and the American Civil War with the volume's presiding theme of surveillance – here, the scrutinising gaze is seen through the early days of photography, the set-piece war painting (Louis Lang's 'Return of the 69th [Irish] Regiment'), which transforms to 'Kodachrome', and the sights of the nearly anachronistic 'sniper'. 'A Civil War Suite' ends, via Whitman and Dickinson, with Sally Mann's overwhelming 'Battlefield' photographs, which are replete with the layers of their own making while also being plain landscapes of Civil War sites. Mann's work (in this series, at least) is analogous in photography to Muldoon's in poetry:

> Less the idea of what the world might be 'like'
> than what it is 'like *photographed*'

The quoted phrase is from Mann, who is in turn paraphrasing Gary Winogrand, and the levels of removal from the 'real', the thing that is plainly in sight, align Mann's artistic methods with Muldoon's. But the American Civil War's resonances in *One Thousand Things Worth Knowing* do not end with Irish allusions, references to other poets, and a photographer whose work parallels Muldoon's. The final, long poem in the volume, 'Dirty Data', pulls on this thread in another way.

'Dirty Data' is a series of nineteen sonnets, with lines which often straggle beyond the right-hand margin and double back on themselves, and which, nevertheless, and with Muldoon's usual jauntiness, retain a Petrarchan rhyme scheme. There is a swirling narrative of sorts, or at least the syntax and grammar of an urgent story, if not the plot to drive it. The poem develops a mode of address to 'Lew', who is Lew Wallace, author of *Ben Hur*. *Ben Hur* is, in turn, 'Irished' into Ben Hourihane, and due note is made that Irish actor Stephen Boyd played Messala in the film version alongside Charlton Heston. If this seems to be merely concatenous serendipity, then we should return to 'A Civil War Suite', in which the photographic and painterly motifs entwine civil conflict and the gaze of surveillance. The American Civil War was the first photographed war. Probably over one million photographs were taken of the conflict. The link with *Ben Hur*, which allows Muldoon to unspool the strands, is that Lew Wallace, author of *Ben Hur*, was also a general in the Union army. *Ben Hur* was, therefore, an allegory of sorts, a novel which used its Romans versus Christians narrative to contemplate mid-nineteenth-century America. And so Wallace is another who is conceptually akin to Muldoon. Wallace's investigation of the failing powers of Rome, combined with the obsessive looking, gazing, visual record-making of the Civil War, then sends Muldoon's poem towards Ireland in a different and more purposeful way – not through amusing coincidence, but through what is the book's most extraordinary and repeated obsession – the early years of the Troubles. The nineteen-sixties and -seventies in Northern Ireland (via Muldoon's youth, Bloody Sunday, the revisitation of his earlier poem 'Cuba', and more) erupt into these poems surrounded by the language of empire, Roman and British, and always with a knowledge of the deadening, deathly and overbearing presence of ideology. The plodding path of Winston Churchill's funeral along the Thames is undertaken on the resonantly named MV *Havengore*, which carried Churchill's coffin and was also the first survey vessel to use computerised data collection. Muldoon's language, his verve and jauntiness, his insistent anachronisms, all fight against the regulation of language, form and meaning. But why, in this volume, are they so focused on Northern Ireland at the beginning of the Troubles?

Muldoon has, of course, always dazzled stern-faced politics with his verse. His apparent circumnavigations of the War in Iraq in *Horse*

Latitudes are an example of how his indirectness can approach political conflict with sure precision. But in *One Thousand Things Worth Knowing* a specific interest in the North is signalled in the first poem in the collection, much discussed since its initial publication, 'Cuthbert and the Otters'. Written in memory of Seamus Heaney (and commissioned for Durham Book Festival), 'Cuthbert and the Otters' interleaves South Shields and Northumbria, at various historical moments, via the Vikings, to Heaney's death and his poetry, while the ideologies which underpin British post-war militarism ('Mountbatten of Burma. Montgomery of Alamein') sound out across the poems. Thinking about Heaney's passing sends Muldoon back to his own origins, again.

Paul Durcan's *The Days of Surprise* also laments the passing of Seamus Heaney, in a tender poem which has Heaney's voice echoing down Durcan's chimney: '"Are you all right down there, Poet Durcan?"' Durcan has no qualms about making Heaney speak and forming Heaney's speech in loping Durcanesque fashion. 'Breaking News' is a beautifully raw poem of love and debt. *The Days of Surprise* is replete with Durcan monologues, either in something approximating his own first-person voice or through *dramatis personae* who are, more often than not, female. In a volume which is bookended by youth and old age, childhood and death, it is the bookends which include the most fulfilling poems. 'Meeting a Neighbour in the GP's Waiting Room' tells the story of 'Durcan' meeting someone he has seen for years, but whom he doesn't know well. In conversation with this 'authentic Victorian Renaissance man', a 'Pre-Raphaelite with iron in his soul', they talk poetry and writing. Their overlapping passions include Heaney, Harry Clifton and Caitríona O'Reilly, and the poem ends with a lament that this new friendship, all boyish and coy, cannot be carried out boyishly:

> Oh, if only I had a home of my own
> I could invite him to come and look at my albums:
> My stamp album, my autograph album, my photograph album!
> As we part at his gate, keeping a straight bat,
>
> He quotes Charles Tomlinson
> With a twinkle in his eye. Charles Tomlinson!

The boy Durcan, meanwhile, is wonderfully imagined in '57 Dartmouth Square', a contemplation of how the co-ordinates of childhood are mapped around the childhood home: 'I was my home, my home was my name'. The inevitable separation ensues ('One day I'd cease to be 57 Dartmouth Square'), and Durcan begins the journey towards becoming 'the happy neurotic I aspired to be'.

The Days of Surprise has its moments of flatness, both in imagination and in writing. When he is directly satiric ('The W.B. Yeats Shopping Centre') there is little enough that the poetry adds to his discomfort with the commercialisation and commodification of culture, or the obvious failings of the Catholic Church ('St Peter's Square, Sunday Morning 27 April 2014'). But when Durcan enters the quotidian, especially that of Dublin of the even-numbered postcodes, the everydayness of the lives his verse inhabits deepens. In 'Visiting Elizabeth at Home – In Beloved Memory: Elizabeth Walsh Peavoy 1945-2014', Elizabeth Peavoy voices the poem and talks about her son, Tadhg:

> The Red Cross gave him wellington boots
> And a set of underwear.
> In the heart of Manitoba.

Rhythmically and imaginatively, this is Durcan at his humane and poetic best, when his ability to be the lightning rod through which 'the Panoply of Human Experience' travels is the source of illumination in his writing.

Jan Wagner

ESSAY ON SOAP

a piece was always close by,
passing through another phase,
lessening like all else,
then it was there again, whole
and dazzling white in its dish.

it weighed like a stone in your fist,
it lathered and softened.
we washed our way from cain to abel.

unused, it disintegrated
into brittle bits of asteroid,
but now it is shiny and wet,

as if fished from the depths
of the lake, treasure for seconds,

and all of us here at the table:
a moonless evening, our fragrant hands.

– translated by **Richard Begbie**

John Gosslee

POST

Everywhere is a birthplace, a pad of paper.

I want to write about the stripped bottles
in the summer garage, the luxury suite over the city.

I wrestle my way back into torn jeans,
blue hair, her star-tattooed shoulders,
how many lifestyle changes make a whole life?

In the story she puts the backpack
in the dryer and stays.

I didn't imagine being so small in the bottle's reflection
pumping on the tide just off shore,
the living don't remember their lovers' hands,
they feel their breath against the ear, taste the salt.

John Gosslee

THE CONGRESS

Music merges with the billboards
that arc into a gristled light around the car.

The bartender is so attentive to the tilt
of the whiskey bottle pouring out its earth.
The librarian's shorthand records
a copper cup next to the five tap beer spout,
the bill footed by the waiter in an apron and bowtie
after the table skips out.

My reflection in the big hotel window
framing the city lights fixed on the grid,
clothed in taxes, hums a song about the now.
The contracts and ornaments don't smooth
the skyline against the dawn.
I hear the keycard click in the slot,
the ice crack when the water hits the glass.

Rachel Coventry

WHAT DID I DO TO DESERVE YOU?

We exist so the universe
can experience loneliness

you may think if everything
is one, it will be content,
there will be no suffering

you are wrong
if there is just one thing
there can only be longing
with nothing to long for

so here we are, splinters
in the dark, no other purpose
but to break each other's hearts.

Katherine Robinson

BORDERLAND

I know why the ocean makes us drunk.
I know why fish are dark
and how small fish become another fish's flesh.
I know how the stag's skin is made
into a bag for mead.
I know how scales cover fish.

I know why the white swan's feet are black.
I know about a four-sided spear; it gave me a terrible wound.
I know why spirits in heaven never break.
I know about four clods of dust,
but I do not know where they will drift,
although I know where the deer and wild boar wander.

And now I greet you, bard,
standing at the border
where bones are made of mist
and two waterfalls of wind meet.

*The poem is a translation of a passage from a Welsh poem, 'Angar Kyfyndawt' /
'The Hostile Confederacy', which is attributed to the bard Taliesin and included
in a medieval manuscript called* The Book of Taliesin. *I have used the version
presented in Marged Haycock's* Legendary Poems From the Book of
Taliesin.

Martin Malone

BITTERSWEET GIFTS

Kate Tempest, *Hold Your Own* (Picador Poetry), £9.99.
George the Poet, *Search Party* (Virgin Books), £9.99.

Hype is something of a poisoned chalice to the artist: on the one hand it
offers the rich pickings of exposure and a ready audience that she would
be mad to disdain; on the other there is often a price to pay in the un-
reasonable levels of expectation, resentment and fair-weather patronage
that accompany it. This year's voice of the urban precariat can so easily
become next year's remaindered stock, its messages unanswered on the
journalist's phone. In pop, rock, rap 'n' roll this has long been the case
but in something that's meant to enjoy a longer shelf-life, like poetry,
how does that work? Thankfully, it's a situation, I suspect, Kate Tempest
won't have to face. I say thankfully because, in approaching her second
full collection *Hold Your Own*, I had to negotiate an initial scepticism born
largely of the sheer volume of coverage Tempest has received during the
past two years, since her epic narrative poem *Brand New Ancients* won the
Ted Hughes Prize in 2013; two years during which she has also released
the excellent *Everybody Down* album and chucked in a couple of plays and
a debut novel for good measure. Added to this were my own ambivalent
feelings towards the spoken-word scene and the suspicion that, at 52, this
stuff isn't meant for me anyway. The girl was playing catch-up, then, and
that wasn't fair. More unfair, however, would have been an easy adoption
of Tempest as some sort of vicarious gate-keeper to the struggles of the
contemporary underclass just in order to appear down with the kids.
There's a lot of it about in the UK and it sucks. What plaudits come her
way here, then, Kate Tempest earns and there are plenty.
    One of the collection's core strengths is the clever use it makes of the
gender-bending Tiresius myth as its main organising principle. Transformed by Hera into a woman, blinded by Athena, granted the bittersweet gift of prophecy, Tiresius provides the perfect mythical sheath for
Tempest's confident handling of the liminal characters, gender identities
and nascent sexualities that slide in and out of the five sequences which
make up her book. Written across the classical tropes is also Tempest's
ongoing alignment with Blakean notions of a primitive *spiritus Brittanicus*
abroad in the streets of Old England-in-the-Now. Indeed, just as Roots
Manuva suggested the aural template that allowed me to tune into *Everybody Down*, it was Blake who provided a spirit guide into this collection;
once I'd gleaned this, *Hold Your Own* started to gather ambition and fearlessness about itself and reveal its considerable strengths. In one sense,

therefore, the collection continues the visionary overhaul of a post-lapsarian urban England begun in *Brand New Ancients*. This visionary element is bulked out by similarly Blakean reminders of the song-like quality present at the heart of poetry, in a poem like the closing 'Prophet', for example, with its sign-off:

> *This old tribe ain't nothing special.*
> *All my life I've watched men wrestle,*
> *Stealing land to fly their flags.*
> He keeps his eyes in a plastic bag.
>
> He keeps his eyes in a plastic bag.

It's in moments like these that Tempest most successfully transfers her spoken-word energies to the page and, in doing so, reminds us that the lilt of song is not so very far from many a classic text which has passed into the canon. Similarly, the Blake of *Songs of Innocence and Experience* is not far away from lines like: 'No flower bends its head to offer / teaching to a seed' from the excellent 'For my niece'. Nor are the Prophetic books too distant from the playful aphorisms of 'These things I know':

> The clever folk talk in endless circles and congratulate themselves on
>   being so untouched by passion.
> But since when did the clever folk ever know anything?

Whilst this may be Tempest getting a bit of retaliation in first, against the perceived sniffiness of some page poets towards spoken-word artists like herself, it is more useful as a reminder that this book works best when its free-wheeling ambition, fearlessness and swagger align it with the vision-ary outsider school it so clearly celebrates. *Hold Your Own*, then, is no collection about art, flowers, or the joys of gardening; it is a polyamorous embrace of growing up, with all the hybridity, danger and experimenta-tion that can involve. Nowhere is this more apparent than in the second section, 'Childhood', which yields what are probably the book's most accessible poems and those most likely to be found in future anthologies: the beautifully realised depiction of 'Bully', the canny re-location of Tiresias's snake incident to contemporary childhood in 'Snakes in the grass', the insider gender politics of 'Thirteen' and the depiction of early sexual-ity in 'Girl next door' will speak to most kids growing up now with the authority of one not long moved on. Similarly, the next section, 'Woman-hood', examines growth and sexual maturation in some memorable and touching poems. Less successful are the formal experiments of the sestina, 'You eat me up and I like it', and the sonnet 'Waking up with you this morning'. But – purists note – *they're here* and where they clunk they only do so in the way many a contemporary effort at an older form does.

Of course there are page moments when the performance energy falls flat; usually when the vocal engine is idling and merely turning over the full-rhymes or when, as in 'The cypher', the poet gets distracted by a badass growth-of-the-rapper thing and comes over all *8 Mile*. Equally, there are moments when lines that would read well in songs don't quite hold their own as poetry on the page (there I've said it) but overall, this book bears the mark of a good editor and a dedicated poet sensible enough to be edited.

From north of the river and tough manors, by way of Cambridge University, comes George The Poet, whom Virgin Books are certainly pitching in the vein of crossover music-scene poets like Linton Kwesi Johnson and Dr John Cooper Clarke. By inclination, I am, as they say, bang into this; though I'd pay good money to see if George could hold his own in a beer and piss-soaked Middlesbrough Rock Garden before a drunken audience of baying Fall fans, as I once saw JCC do. It's not like I'm not a sympathetic audience, but I confess to being disappointed. When the mission statement and endorsements take up a lot of the cover and opening pages, it usually means that what follows is either going to struggle to match up or be something pretty darn special (see opening point about hype). Unfortunately, here I just couldn't see (or hear) what I was being told I was looking at.

Perhaps it's less George The Poet's fault than that of an over-eager publishing scene too willing to provide such a well-dressed platform to someone with impeccable credentials and obvious talent, but who, with the best will in the world, is not quite ready yet. This collection just screamed out for a good editor to slow down the relentless flow of full-rhyme and big abstractions, and help the poet switch pace or escape the polemical comfort-zone that a lot of spoken-word artists cosy up to. In a short piece like 'Ride Out', for example, I counted eight big abstract concepts in a nine-line poem. The ephemeral flow of live performance allows you to go with the rhythmic energy of such words but, naked on the page, you just want to take a pencil to them.

In poems like the excellent 'His Mistakes' (a benevolent address to the young son of a single mum) George The Poet is addressing a truly important issue of our time: the absence of positive male role models from the lives of way too many young boys. This poem models a subtlety of rhythm, rhyme and insight which I was genuinely hoping to encounter more often than I did. Lines like ...

> So he pays a heavy price for his mistakes.
> So heavy each shoulder's numb.

He knows it's dumb, but for your sake he holds his tongue
And holds a grudge. He holds it within
With no release, until he's old enough to go to the gym

... encapsulate the sort of subtle interplay of pronouns, half-rhyme,
internal rhyme and male motivation that show where this collection *could*
have gone with a little more discipline or judicious editing. As it was, I
got more and more frustrated: as George himself observes by the later
poem 'YOLO', 'All my poems are starting to sound the same.' Maybe
these are my problems, not his. However, I can fault neither aspiration
nor intended audience when George The Poet cuts to the chase:

I want higher educational achievement for marginalised groups.
I gotta target the right youts.

– 'ELEPHANT KNOWS'

If he hits his target – to 'Make them understand what happens in the ends'
– then who am I stand in his way?

Štěpán Nosek

THE POND – MOONLIGHT, 1904

Do as I say. Kick your shoes off into the reeds and enter the glassy water, blackest and most viscous at the edge. You feel the oily patterns of bright granules drawn to your calves; your shadow, fallen backwards into the lattice and the twinkling dust; the sticky dizziness beneath your feet; the sweet stifled vertigo. And now lean forward a bit, touch the surface with your fists and immerse your hands until they penetrate the light blue leaves pressed together underwater. Then slowly relax, open your fingers as wide as you can, until you feel the pull between them, until the edges of vascular blades tingle in your palms. Until you feel a stabbing in your shoulders. Stay like that for a while. And endure it even longer. Wait to feel what happens, how it slowly passes, how it begins to abate, lose its colour, flow out along stems rooted in the darkness, float away on the bodies of imaginary fish. Don't move yet. Wait until your body loses feeling. Then come back out onto the shore. When you turn around, you will see that trap. The moon has disentangled itself from the branches. The surface has dulled like a bog puddle coated with morning frost. An impassive calm pearly disk. A mirror turned downward. And that which was rippling, which has been rocking the plaits of the waterweeds, which churns the sludge and shines olive, is the obverse side, separate, beneath it, foreign, there – now just an echo, a background, lines, nature.

– translated by **Kirsten Lodge**

Štěpán Nosek

'IN THE SUNLIT GARDEN'

in the sunlit garden
the screen is a dusty mirror

I must shield it to read
that you live in constant rain and cold

and nothing can be done
I don't believe it

from the ash tree's dark interior
the sound of welling water

– translated by **Kirsten Lodge**

Patrick Moran

BULBS

It was (I dreamt) years from now.
My father had long since died, and memories
of him, so vivid once, were fading:
the man whose deft touch could rouse
a sluggish fire; whose fingers knew
the inner workings of clocks and watches;
but most, the inveterate sower of seed,
so indulgent he'd let stray lettuces
or spuds flourish in a drill of carrots;
who, even when stooped with age, could still wonder:
Where do all the weeds come out of?
This stubborn man whose gifts I didn't have,
whose paths I wouldn't follow.

So there I was, standing
on a neglected patch of ground,
not knowing why: Instinct? The lengthening
evenings? A bird's lingering notes?
And I didn't seem to know what to set:
Flowers? Shrubs? Organic vegetables?

I was just getting down to work,
turning scraws over with a spade,
when I came on them, snug as landmines: bulbs
he'd planted years before, still waiting there ...

Innocent, helpless, strangely eloquent.

Ian Harrow

GARDEN VIEW

Love, I hardly know you
from what I never had.

I suppose I must have gone too far,
tying the weeks and the months in knots,
thinking it right for the time, but love
you have fallen somewhere between
what was expected
and the glad-to-be-gone.

Instead of some all-day, all-night drive,
I sit with empty hands and heart,
with a garden view of the rooks
that are blown, no distance, into rags.

Seán Lysaght

NARCISSUS

Smell and colour in a house
ruled by hyacinth are such

that we forget to look out
until a casual glance finds

a first bloom under the alders
beating its head in a gale –

beating, beating on a peg
where day clings and cloud-wars pass.

It has no pond to study,
nothing you could call a face

skittering off a raindrop.
Its best mirror is the O of time.

In the empty, waning
room of winter

it spins the thread of itself
so thinly, like a dancer

staging a part on its own
before spring opens.

(Players are already in the wings,
but it is oblivious to them).

Then, the only night
falls, for all it knows,

suddenly calm, with a big moon
establishing trees and the house

in a setting of moon shadows.

James Conor Patterson

BAMBOOLAND

As one put drunk into the back of a parent's car –
seized, it would seem, by the adolescent desire

to be reminded of one's failings – this morning
saw me return to Bambooland near John Martin Gardens.

I went alone, spurred as I had been in previous years
by the cousin who supplied the Sprite bottle-lung, the beer,

the suite of cobbled furniture pilfered out of skips.
Back then we'd sit for hours atop broken doors & pallets

until one of us, suddenly compelled to danger,
would gaze square into the bamboo void and bid the other,

'Jump!' as though nothing at all would stop us;
as though neither one had thought, like Orpheus,

that to descend in order to retrieve might leave us
head-propped against the lyre – might see us

ascend again with scuffmarks wound beneath the skin,
and trailed by the scents of bamboo, oak & whin.

Damien French

AUTUMN LEAVES

The air's graze
In a wide clearing
Under a ripe sky.

Hints in the lines
Of these trees, around me,
In this windy square.

How the leaves flap
And tumble
With useless litter.

How much have I
To let drop
In this wind

Until I am as kind
As the sunlight
That strikes the bare branches?

David McLoghlin

A TRANSATLANTIC MENAGERIE: THE ANIMAL POETRY OF BISHOP,
LOWELL, HEANEY AND GRENNAN

One literary pleasure – for writers as well as readers – that maybe isn't
mentioned as much as it should be is the kind of influence that stems
from affection rather than anxiety and is not a burden. A good example
is the 'chain letter' between two American poets, Elizabeth Bishop and
Robert Lowell, that was later glossed, or added to, by two Irish poets of a
younger generation: namely, Eamon Grennan and Seamus Heaney.

It has long been known that, as part of their mammoth correspondence, Bishop and Lowell wrote and dedicated poems to each other (*Words
in Air*, their complete letters, runs to 795 pages).[1] Bishop started the pro-
cess with 'The Armadillo' from Brazil in 1957.[2] Apart from the strangeness
of a landscape where 'almost every night / the frail, illegal fire balloons
appear', and the beauty of lines like 'the kite sticks of the Southern Cross',
what is curious in Bishop's poem is just how brief an appearance the
armadillo makes in a poem named after it; once it eventually appears, it
gets only three lines:

> Hastily, all alone,
> a glistening armadillo left the scene,
> rose-flecked, head down, tail down ...

This could be due to the rarity of armadillo sightings, even in a place as
unspoiled as Samambaia, the village outside Petrópolis where Bishop
lived with her lover, Lota de Macedo Soares, forty-five miles north of Rio
de Janeiro. It's more interesting, though, to consider the shy armadillo
in terms of the bestiary that Bishop uses to express her own submerged
sense of anxiety and spiritual homelessness – 'The Sandpiper', for example,
is constantly on alert, and nervous of the world: 'He runs, he runs to
the south, finical, awkward, / in a state of controlled panic, a student of
Blake.'[3]

Lowell responded with 'Skunk Hour', from a macabre 1957
Massachusetts where 'My mind's not right.'[4] In a letter from September
11, 1957, he writes: 'There's one in a small voice ... called "Skunk Hour",
not in your style yet indebted a little to your "Armadillo".'[5] Contrast
Bishop's armadillo with Lowell's skunk family, who 'march on their
soles up Main Street: / white stripes, moonstruck eyes' red fire'. Lowell's
animals populate a more confident anthropomorphic environment.

From the point of view of an interplay between traditions, what is in a
sense more unexpected is the way Eamon Grennan and Seamus Heaney

pay homage to Lowell's and Bishop's influence by dipping their toes in American waters in their own animal poems. 'The Skunk' by Heaney appeared in *Field Work* in 1979; Grennan's 'Towards Dusk the Porcupine' was published in *So It Goes* in 1995.[6]

As he mentions in *Stepping Stones* – the autobiography-via-interview conducted with the late Dennis O'Driscoll – Heaney was house-sitting for friends in North Berkeley, California, when he had his first encounter. Told by the house's owners 'to look out for this skunk and her family', Heaney is immediately reminded of Lowell's 'mother skunk with her column of kittens'.[7] However, it's vital to consider what Heaney does with this influence. As Michael Cavanagh has noted in *Professing Poetry: Seamus Heaney's Poetics*, ' "The Skunk" doesn't simply borrow from or allude to "Skunk Hour"; it is an answer to that poem, a rival vision of things, a place where Heaney doesn't suggest or declare, but enacts his independence.'[8] The American context, 'the night earth and air // Of California', doesn't continue to evoke Lowell for Heaney, but instead brings to mind his wife's absence:

> The beautiful, useless
> Tang of eucalyptus spelt your absence.
> The aftermath of a mouthful of wine
> Was like inhaling you off a cold pillow.

Despite the hypnotic beauty of his delivery, what is interesting is the way 'The Skunk' – as one of those rare breaks from an Irish context – illuminates Heaney's generative, Antaeus-like focus on Ireland and its countryside. Though clearly showing an enjoyment of 'parts foreign', his imagination doesn't linger in this setting.

Where Bishop begins with a poem about being elsewhere – and making her home there – Lowell responds with a work about the estrangement of home. Heaney, although responding to Lowell's skunks, chimes in with Bishop by thinking of home while abroad – the 'transatlantic cable that connected' him to his wife[9] – the skunk's tail evoking the 'tail-up hunt in a bottom drawer / For the black plunge-line nightdress'. In the end, the dalliance with America only reminds him of where his true loyalties lie. Finally, Grennan returns to the poetic communion between Bishop and Lowell – not necessarily via Heaney, though he would have been aware of Heaney's 'Skunk' and its echoes of Lowell.

In 'Towards Dusk the Porcupine', Grennan completely enters the scene (rather like Bishop does in 'The Fish'). The way in which the context is not overly noted as American, or fetishized as different, might reflect the fact that Grennan has lived in the United States since 1964, and might not view his environs as foreign. (Though, I appreciate the gusto of

Hibernian touches like 'the targe of his arse'). The poem's close-up eye on the porcupine reflects the immediacy of the encounter. Typical of Grennan, although the poem has four full stops, it reads as if it unspooled in a single breath – one sentence, expertly syntactically sustained, winding through the tercets. Though the 'I' is only present as a vehicle for the moment captured in the poem, rather wonderfully, we are given the poet from the porcupine's perspective as 'this small walking tree at which / he nods once a bobbing head and then / goes deeper in, to be lost'.

Quills as writing instruments suggests the porcupine to be the writer's mascot *par excellence*, and indeed the porcupine's armature is punned on to great effect. Here, 'one brilliant quill of curiosity' stands in for 'shooting a glance'. Preceding these stanzas, the porcupine is described 'peering shortsighted / / at the ground he's covering / hunched over – like Lowell reading'. And, a nod to Lowell's nickname – Cal – comes in the ninth stanza, where the porcupine is envisioned 'doing this undulant / slow waddle – fat Caliban'. (Per Lowell: 'I'm called Cal, but I won't explain why. None of the prototypes are flattering: Calvin, Caligula, Caliban').[10] Finally, and beautifully, after the porcupine's noticing his own prickliness, 'how / he ends at pointed edges like that / / and can cast them off / when needs be', we are given 'his heart / in its reed basket / / a full thumping, the twenty / species of beetle and seed / sweetening his belly'.

Grennan's work is often a question of travel (travel also involves extended, decades-long stays, and I believe in this Bishop would approve). As such, his poems move expertly between Ireland and America. A vein in Grennan's work uncannily captures the emigrant experience by bleeding both landscapes in a single poem, echoing the mind's jet lag in a kind of melancholy double exposure. If at times Irish poets can tend too often to see landscape and fauna in historical terms, Grennan is a restorative: in many poems he gives us the sharply focused 'moment of being' in a painterly mode that is perhaps more American than Irish. (The eye, arguably, might be younger in the United States). In this he shows a new way of being an Irish poet, and one who has been fully received and welcomed by the American scene: maintaining a dual poetic citizenship, while keeping his passport to an honoured place in his original tradition.

Just as Lowell absorbs Bishop's approach and mise-en-scène by responding with something of his own, Grennan and Heaney cleanly integrate the older poets by taking what they need to make their own non-derivative poems. In this way they pay the taxes that are due as they pass through customs, but also show the necessary confidence inherent to mature poets of stature. Where Heaney's visits Stateside did not tend to register quite so forcefully again in his work, Grennan's work has grown out of this transatlantic conversation.

Footnotes

Unless noted, any reference is to the specific poems under discussion: 'The Armadillo', 'Skunk Hour', 'The Skunk' and 'Towards Dusk the Porcupine'.

1. *Words in Air: The Complete Correspondence Between Elizabeth Bishop and Robert Lowell* (Farrar, Straus and Giroux, 2010), edited by Thomas Travisano with Saskia Hamilton.
2. Elizabeth Bishop, *Poems* (Farrar, Straus and Giroux, 2011).
3. Elizabeth Bishop, *Poems*.
4. Robert Lowell, *Life Studies and For the Union Dead* (Farrar, Straus and Giroux Classics, 2007).
5. *Words in Air*, p. 230.
6. Seamus Heaney, *Field Work* (Faber and Faber, 1979); Eamon Grennan, *So it Goes* (The Gallery Press, 1995).
7. Dennis O'Driscoll, *Stepping Stones: Interviews with Seamus Heaney* (Faber and Faber, 2009), p. 205.
8. Michael Cavanagh, *Professing Poetry: Seamus Heaney's Poetics* (Catholic University of America Press, 2010), pp. 137-138.
9. *Stepping Stones*, p. 205.
10. *Words in Air*, p. 7.

'Torn Sky': **Dominic Turner** (www.dominicturner.ie)

'Along the Garavogue, 1': **Sheila McSweeney** (sheilamcsweeney@gmail.com)

'Early Morning, The Gasworks': **Fergus Bourke**, 1934–2004 (www.fergusbourke.org)

'Arashiyama': **Hugh O'Conor** (www.hughoconor.com)

'The Cellar chats of Paris': **John Minihan** (http://johnminihan.blogspot.ie)

Thanks to So Fine Art Editions, 10 South Anne St, D2 (**www.sofinearteditions.com**),
for providing these photographs from the 'Shutter' summer 2016 exhibition
(**www.sofinearteditions.com/shutter**)

Robert Colman

WHERE WE TAKE IT

Nearly hit a porcupine last night
but I was thirty-ish safe on the straight lanes
and the wind fierced me quiet in the swerve.

I'd found our road, which surprised you.
Dark was dark, and the trees were sleeping.

Earlier, you had imagined mafia making rough in a Camaro
and I was liking the open road less and less.
I took on the threat, gave it an engine, wondered where next.

The town shunted its hull lakeside,
a harbourmaster's bottled shout.

The rain was warm. No need to change
our clothes or even run
for cover.

So we stayed the same
just as the day started.

Gabriella Attems

LAST CLIMB

You might be skilled at finding doors
but these stairs go past mine. Next time
you visit, I'll house you in the topmost
room, hemmed in by clouds.

Because all I'd like to do with you
in the morning is find that raven's nest
up on the crag. We'll climb the overhang
toes and fingers stretched without
looking down at the stream.

I won't distract you, I know the rock
is loose to your left and the drop clean.

Ben McGuire

AN EARLIEST JOURNEY I CAN REMEMBER

Was this mine? Half
detective work to remember
bits of childhood but it
must have been for a holiday
somewhere. So,
here's the colossal car,
here's my ridgy seatbelt.
They're in front,
steering grey out to green –
his curls, and her wide hair.
She turns round to me,
asks if I'm alright. I think I am.

John Kinsella

PATHS TO THE WURMLINGER CHAPEL

The cut logs piled and numbered – wood raddled –
alongside the paths, twist the blade into the spirit
of forest, however foresters are trying to reinvent

the primeval. A woodpecker cranks up intensity
and shelf fungus on a stump declaims to the under-
storey; moss treats the wounds of older stumps

but fresh bloody stumps smell sickly sweet, conifer
and deciduous ichor blending at a time when budding
still works, comes basically on song. Where smooth snakes

awoken will crackle through winter-dried leaves, vapid
in the awakening. Ravenousness will come to the Spitzberg
soon, and wild boar will charge from the hollows.

So down to the fruit trees and grapevines on terraces
to climb again against the flow of mountain bikes
exaggerating every step and erosion, to bring

it to the extreme sport variation on stations,
the seventeenth-century chapel crowning off,
canopy, its medieval crypt into the breast

of the mount, four-hundred-and-seventy-five metres'
elevation of panorama: of villages and motorways, of haze
and a coal tit outrageously loud. Where the dead

rest on high and Uhland's poem of a young shepherd below,
the dead going to ground up in the blue gleam,
and where he will go too when life finishes its dirge.

Nessa O'Mahony

MARATHON MEN, MARATHON WOMEN

Eiléan Ní Chuilleanáin, *The Boys of Blue Hill* (The Gallery Press, 2015), €11.95.
Frank Ormsby, *Goat's Milk: New and Selected Poems* (Bloodaxe Books, 2015), £12.
Gerard Smyth, *A Song of Elsewhere* (Dedalus Press, 2015), €11.50.

The opening lines of 'Some Older American Poets', from Frank Ormsby's *Goat's Milk: New and Selected Poems*, offer a pithy summary of the three volumes under consideration here:

> Tired of the accomplished young men
> and the accomplished young women,
> their neat cerebral arcs and sphinctral circles,
> their impeccable chic, their sudden precocious surge,
> their claims to be named front-runner,
> I have turned to the ageing poets – the marathon men,
> the marathon women – the ones who breasted the tape
> and simply ran on, establishing their own distance.

In an era when the latest arrivals seem to eclipse so much, it is refreshing to be reminded that excellence was not invented by a generation born in the 1980s.

Indeed, reading these three poets' latest volumes together reinforces a sense of indebtedness. Between them, Eiléan Ní Chuilleanáin, Gerard Smyth and Frank Ormsby have produced no fewer than eighteen volumes of poetry, have edited or co-edited some of the most influential outlets for poetry in Ireland as well as some of the most significant anthologies of the past four decades, and have contributed significantly to the critical canon of Irish literature. And somehow they have still found time to craft poetry of heart-stilling beauty.

In *The Boys of Bluehill*, Ní Chuilleanáin offers a series of dramatic tableaux in which a memory of some past event is reappraised in an effort to achieve some fresh sense of understanding of the present. She often presents the speaker pressed up against a window or at a portal of some kind, looking in at shadows of the past, as in the poem 'Stabat Mater', where 'you can only find out by pushing / forward in the crowd / until your body is pressed / flat against the glass'. The reward for that effort is the chance to experience once again 'the elation / of the strings, their long hopping', an almost Wordsworthian recapturing of an emotion long lost.

Ní Chuilleanáin offers no easy clues to the context of each meditation; the poems often feel like Renaissance paintings, where the mood is evoked through the precise details of the imagery and the clues they suggest. Things are in a protean state: indeed there are a number of references to Proteus in this collection. In 'Who Were Those Travellers', change is evoked thus:

> Something has intervened, they are not
> elemental as before, exile has changed them;
>
> they are thin as air, as a leaf that has stayed
> a century inside a book.

The just-so-ness of that leaf simile is utterly characteristic of her work, as is the sense of past resonances it evokes.

Personas are sometimes presented, yet they feel more archetypal than real, as for example in 'The Orchestra Again', where the dream-like opening image of 'a helmet floating / half sunk in the mountain pool' is followed by a line of speech: *'Could that have been his, she wondered.'* Who the 'she' is, or how she relates to the speaker, is not explained. And though the second section of the poem presents us with an 'I' and a more direct address, we remain unclear about the relationships contained here, though utterly convinced by the sense of a connection that once was and that continues to be waited for.

Gerard Smyth's poetry feels less liminal, though his nocturnal wanderings in *A Song of Elsewhere* share a similar concern to reconnect with the past or to ensure that it is not lost. The landscapes moved through are more concrete: actual streetscapes of brick and mortar, treaded upon by the poet and the generations that both precede and come after him, as in 'The Starting-Place', where he walks through 'haunts / that remind me of who I was', or 'Summer Nocturne', where 'in random places we find last vestiges / of a filling station or a parish hall / / that used to be the destination of travelling-players'. The poet is constantly on the move in this collection, celebrating fellow travellers, lamenting those who are gone.

Both Ní Chuilleanáin and Smyth include elegies for artists and poets with the former's moving laments for Pearse Hutchinson and Eamonn O'Doherty complimented by Smyth's elegies for Seamus Heaney and Francis Harvey. Smyth's poem 'Bounty' is a vivid and tender capturing of his former *Irish Times* colleague, the late Caroline Walsh:

> And here's a memory in different colours,
> your laugh that showered its sparks on us,
> red lipstick on the rim of a coffee cup
>
> or your straw bag stuffed with pages
> of revisions to the countless ways of telling a story ...

There is also the faintest echo of another fallen comrade; Smyth shares Dennis O'Driscoll's mordant humour, the scepticism that records our tendency to commodify history and airbrush out the darker aspects. In the poem 'Islandbridge' he offers the juxtaposition of picnic tables and a war memorial, while in 'Wings of Desire' he notes that 'Over the traces of Kristallnacht, / they have built the fashionable streets'.

Frank Ormsby's interest in history is of a more personal kind, though politics is never far away, as *Goat's Milk,* which includes selections from his first four collections, along with forty-six new poems, testifies. Throughout his career he returns poetically to the small farm in Fermanagh where he grew up and where he first experienced loss: his father's stroke and eventual death are a recurring subject. But Ormsby, like Kavanagh before him, sees the universal in the parochial, and produces carefully honed, unerringly accurate depictions, capturing, as Michael Longley puts it in his introduction to the book, 'something desolate and unsettling [that] shades this poet's vision'. Longley quotes Ormsby's own definition of the lyric poem as an illustration of his 'ars poetica', and it encapsulates well the techniques on display here: 'an insight distilled or crystallised, the essence of a mood or emotion caught with memorable concision, the verbal equivalent – linguistic, aphoristic, epigrammatic – of the brushstroke'.

The earliest poems suggest a debt to Kavanagh in their ability to evoke the rural world in concrete detail, where 'small ads give notice of a world / where little is wasted' (in 'The Practical Farms', from the first collection, *A Store of Candles*) and where nothing, not even milk churns and steel cans, is beneath the poet's notice because he is capturing the universal through the 'sadness of dim places, obscure lives', as he puts it in another early poem, 'Landscape with Figures'. But the characteristics of that first collection, the detailed and accurate portraits of local characters, the slanted take on sectarian divides (in poems such as 'Sheepman') and the painfully beautiful elegies in poems such as 'A Day in August' – 'And now the wheels are turning. They impress / tracks that will not outlast the winter's rain' – remain remarkably consistent throughout his career.

It is shape and form that undergo the greatest changes over the decades. The poems from *The Ghost Train*, his 1995 collection, feel more expansive and meditative, although the focus is still on the familial and the local. Here we get some rare experiments with formal poetry, though he appears less comfortable with the repetitive constraints that villanelles such as 'The Graveyard School' represent. This collection includes the marvellous 'Lullaby', which rivals Muldoon's 'Sonogram' in its tender depiction of an unborn child. The selection from the most recent collection, *Fireflies* (from 2009), features some American poems, including the one quoted at the start of this review, but though in a New World, he rarely loses sight of old concerns with mortality, as poems such as the extended 'Valhalla Journal' sequence demonstrate. The latest poems are shorter, more intense lyrics, some almost haiku-like in their brevity. But they retain Ormsby's eye for detail, his ability to see the numinous in the every day, as 'Bog Cotton' illustrates:

> They have the look
> of being born old.
> Thinning elders among the heather,
> trembling in every wind.

Ormsby's influence on Northern Irish poetry is considerable; indeed, so intense is the anxiety of influence experienced by younger Ulster poets in his regard that he has become the subject of no fewer than two fake Twitter accounts; no greater tribute could the current generation of 'accomplished young men / and the accomplished young women' pay to a senior poet.

Michael Lauchlan

NOW THAT HE'S GONE

forget his ragged return
by way of Niko's Corner Bar
after the bastards hustled him
from the office with a box
of what – photos, a dying plant.
Recall instead what you must
imagine: how that night his wife
let him in and held him
while he couldn't speak, then
when he wouldn't stop and how,
when he was finally still,
she touched him, doing again
in that place, at that hour,
the quiet work of love.

John Hennessy

FAMILY STORY / *SO WHAT DAD*

In the family story, Dad's the first to college.
Five kids and nineteen years of three jobs later
he finishes a Ph.D. And shortly thereafter
goes solo. Our story starts in the New World
several times, most recently with the arrival
of his grandmother, Margaret Kinnane, from Lisdoonvarna,
County Clare. That town's heaven for singles,
cash cow for matchmakers. Every September
thousands of seekers cross the petrified Burren,
coming from all over Europe, all over the world,
to consult with marriage brokers. (New days
in the Old Country: recently The Outing,
a gay weekend, was added). Beautiful in its rainwashed
way, the sun sudden on Norman ruins, Georgian stone,
but still my love teases: plaster Cupids aim
arrows over pub doorways, neon hearts blink
in shop windows. No surprise we ended up
on the Jersey Shore. Margaret came as a domestic,
fourteen years old; she took the family's single
boat ticket when her older sister lost her nerve
at the docks. We called her The Pit Bull – even I
knew her, she lied about her age, but lived late
into the 20th century – and we called her last
husband The Pussycat. My father refused
to go to her funeral, payback, decades after
she jilted her first husband, the Hennessy,
a bartender in Brooklyn, while he wasted in hospital,
dying slowly from an icepick in the eye.

But that's only our most recent arrival story.
My father's other grandmother was a Kettle,
and her folks immigrated earlier. Recently
her family came to us to fill in branches
in their tree, and there were a few surprises.
Grandmother Kettle's family owned farmland

So what if your father
doesn't call you back,
if you don't tell him
about your raise, or the play
your son wrote and directed,
or even the high school
stagehand who called him faggot
and offered to beat him
in the stairwell – your precious boy –
or the fury you stifled (your father's)
to let him as he insisted
handle his own affairs (and has he
even had any yet?),
how you didn't
call the principal, or better park your car
and wait after school for the punk
to walk by so you could threaten him –
remember that childhood truncheon,
your souvenir Mets bat?
This is what you'll get
if it happens again,
in your quietest Jersey voice.
So what if you kept and still keep shtum,
good for you, and your Jersey voice,
which after all isn't a Brooklyn Irish
waterfront naze like his
but your own hangover
from those days of keeping it quiet
and mean and scared
in the liquor store parking lot
behind your old building after he'd
shoved you back outside to fight your own
damned fights, that milling of older kids
from Shotwell Park you insisted
on pitching to, so what if you lifted

in Artane, were thick with Parnell even after
O'Shea's betrayal, agitated in the Land War
and suffered imprisonment at Naas
and again at Kilmainham, ran guns
from Belgium to the Irish Volunteers in '14.
In the middle of it all is Tom Kettle,
the only person James Joyce would talk Aquinas
with, from Clongowes Wood right through
to UCD. An MP, professor, and poet. Statue
in Stephen's Green: he died in 1916. Not
in the Easter Rising, but at the Somme.
He fought the Germans in an Irish regiment
of the British Army and worried he'd be
remembered as a traitor. In our family story
he never went to school or to war, never wrote
a book, held a gun. We would have saved him
from being remembered at all.

a chunk of the rotting tarmac
and hit a kid older by a couple years
in the neck with it, far as you could reach,
so what if you came home
bleeding through your crewcut
and your father took you to Stewart's
for a root beer float
to celebrate? So what if he
doesn't call you back, so what?
Just as the sun
rises on your son he's proud
of you, he's all orange neon
diamonds and soda
and sticky picnic tables,
and the hornets
buzzing for you.
Or text him. Uncork champagne emoji.

Michael Coady

THE JOCK

That's street lingo for cancer hereabouts;
veiled monosyllable, both sharp and blunt,
always with the definite article,
a tone of fatalism and pity

for the stricken. It's a generic code
unspoken in consulting room or ward
but traded in the pub or betting shop.
The jock. It's mouthed softly, perhaps from

our spooked image of an unself within
that might stir awake and mount you bareback
to ride out all the way, nor ever spare
the spurs or bridle, bit or riding crop.

Still, some unseat it. Others go on down
with courage like a sanctifying grace.
That trumpet player, longstanding sideman
through all those nights and places, scores and songs –

recall the final evening he contrived
to haul himself upright and eyeball death,
sip at a beer and manage broken breath
enough to sing with you *As Time Goes By.*

Alice Miller

FOUND WANTING

It's said the last letter written
by the deceased
was found in the garden.
But I've seen men write in his hand before.
And I've heard men do him in different voices.
In this age the most dangerous thing
is to listen and I know if I read the letter
I wouldn't know whose voice it was I heard.
Even now, I do not know him well enough.
Even now, I can't open the envelope.
Even now, a dead man knows more
of what it is I've lost.

Kim Moore

ALL THE MEN I NEVER MARRIED
   NO. 8

It's just me and him, alone in the staffroom
and he's talking about a woman he hates.

I bet she has a big pubic mound. I bet
she's covered in spiders legs.

He's already on about the next thing wrong
with his life, with his job, with this woman

he works with, while I think about the women
I know, how excellent they are at getting rid

of things, experts in the endurance of pain.
Look at me now for example, sitting here

not moving a muscle as I remember
the first morning I took a razor to my face,

because the boys at school called me names,
my mum saying *What have you done?*

Once you start you can't go back.
There was bleach of course, the flame

of it burning my skin, testing myself,
how long could I stand it, how much

could I make disappear. The worst
was electrolysis, a tiny needle inserted

into each follicle and one dark hair
at a time wished away.

Back in the staffroom
he's telling me the next time someone

annoys me I should flash my tits,
miming the action while making a cuppa.

Milk, no sugar, I say with a smile
I hate myself for. I remember the times

I heard that as a teenager: *Get your tits out
for the lads.* It sounds obscene now

but back then it was nothing, just one
of those things that boys said.

In my first class of the morning
a small boy asks why I have hair

on my lip and my stomach
still drops like it used to but I answer

calmly this time. *All women do.
Your mum probably does.* He looks

outraged, and how can I blame him?
This is what we're teaching our sons.

Kim Moore

ALL THE MEN I NEVER MARRIED
   NO. 15

Remember that night we'd been out drinking
and on the way home heard raised voices,

saw a couple across the road, arguing, leaning
towards each other and then he slapped her,

once, across the face then turned and walked away.
She stood there for a while and then she followed,

down Rawlinson Street as the lights from passing cars
fell on her, then swept on by. We didn't call out

or phone the police. We didn't speak, not to her
or him or to each other. When we got home

we didn't talk about the woman in the denim skirt,
holding her white shoes by the straps. I wasn't

close enough to see her feet, yet I remember them,
the blackened soles from walking on the pavement,

the sore on the heel where the strap had rubbed
and raised a patch of red. We did not speak of her

and so we made her disappear, limping into the night,
trying to keep up with that man, who knew she'd follow

so did not turn around, hands thrust into his jeans,
front door key hot between his fingers.

Paul Maddern

ATTENTIONS PAID

Michael McKimm, *Fossil Sunshine* (Worple Press, 2013), £7.
Fiona Benson, *Bright Travellers* (Jonathan Cape, 2014), £10.
Tom French, *Midnightstown* (The Gallery Press, 2014), €11.95.

Michael McKimm's debut collection, *Still This Need* (Heaventree Press, 2009), received scant attention, and that's a pity. He is one of the most interesting Irish writers to emerge in recent years, and those who encountered the debut were struck by his precise and inventive imagery and his disdain of poetic affectation. *Fossil Sunshine* exhibits these same traits and serves to confirm the early promise.

McKimm works for the Geological Society of London. 'Fossil sunshine' is a phrase from the first of six 'Abstract from a Conference' poems, inspired by the publication of papers on the Anthropocene – a term coined to cover the period during which humans have impacted significantly on the Earth's environment. The fourth in the series, with its arresting list structure, is evidence of McKimm's willingness to experiment with form and to question the very nature of poetry. Others in the sequence are typical of the lyrical grace that is such an attractive feature of his work. Number five, in its entirety:

> Know the oceans
> are being altered
>
> the nature of the seafloor
> will change
>
> cream-coloured
> calcium carbonate
>
> dissolved to darker clays

The opening poem, 'Tertiary Basalts', is set in North Antrim, where McKimm was raised, and it makes clear the area's impact on his interest in the natural world: 'They gave to me more pictures than the clouds.' As occurs throughout the collection, the geologist's lexis is employed to great effect but is more than decoration or scientific shorthand; it is part of the poetry:

> Today, where the rope-bridge
> swings over banded ash and basalt bomb, land
> opens south as remnant plug and cinder cone

Elsewhere, McKimm ruminates on a pipeline in Alberta, Gulf Oil spills and visiting geologic sites in Devon, Surrey and East Yorkshire. 'Holderness Boulder Clay' charts a year of wildlife activity and erosion near Bridlington and, as is typical, celebrates the beauty of the landscape while underscoring the potential violence of Man and Nature:

> then scorching August, creaking
> in the air, a good half metre crumbles
> with a Scafell thud. A man out
> with his trowel, checking silt grains
> on his tongue, measures with his eyes
> the tide's new reach, the Millennium
> defences now they're breached.

McKimm's abilities as a poet are evident in this one small passage: the arresting use of Scafell (referencing a famous climbing disaster); the acoustic chimes throughout; and the 'breaching' enjambment – at odds with the controlled rhythms within each line. McKimm's ecological warnings go far beyond polemic: this work is to be enjoyed both for its arguments and its artistry.

Bridlington is the setting for 'Field Notes' (cf., 'Glanmore Sonnets' of *Field Work*), and suggests more than geologic influence at work. McKimm is surely acknowledging the master maker, and his four sonnets follow Heaney's Shakespearean model and confirm his deft handling of metre:

> Going further back, we see then how the land
> in fact curved west away from Bridlington,
> and where we took the rocks, the cliff we walked,
> did not exist, was low Cretaceous chalk.

Fiona Benson made a dramatic entrance onto the poetry scene as a Faber pamphleteer but, incredulously, was not picked up by that publisher for her debut collection, *Bright Travellers*. If Faber is currently captivated by poets involved with sociolinguistic experimentation, perhaps it is best that Benson is with Jonathan Cape – and given the traditions to which it is indebted, it is unsurprising the debut won the Seamus Heaney Centre's First Collection Prize.

Bright Travellers is divided into sections on Devon (where Benson lives), Vincent Van Gogh's lover, poems about miscarriage, and finishes with poems celebrating birth. In the opening sequence, 'Dumnonia',

Benson, like McKimm, digs into the landscape. And there is much darkness and decay. In the opening poem a forest is submerged at the water's edge, with 'dank, eroded beds / of peat-stained oak, pocked / with vanished colonies of whelk'. In 'Clapper Bridge', Benson retreats under the ancient bridge to seek illumination of the dark: 'water-light, / that dance, that luminous flux / and the fraction's shift / in the bedrock of the moor'. 'Urn-burial' concerns the disquieting discovery in a church of the 'quarried hearts [of crusaders] / sent home to roost'.

This pervasive womb-like darkness links to the terrible loss of a child, best evidenced in 'Cave Bear', in which the fossilized remains of a mother bear reveal that her last act was nuzzling the 'crooked skull' of her cub. The poem ends with the image of the broken, dying mother still raging in the subterranean dark:

> till you are a vault
> for the one clear thought
> of your life:
>
> the cub is dead.
> You show your teeth
> as the massive slab
> of your heart
> gives way.

This is controlled and subtle: the brilliance of the mother as the evidential 'vault' of devotion; the tragedy augmented by that stanza break; the clever enjambment of the final four lines, providing a heartbreaking yet defiant finish; and the sheer beauty of the present tense to suggest eternal anguish.

Loss is handled with great care and often surprising results. 'Sheep' juxtaposes that animal with her stillborn lambs and the human mother observing this scene from bed. She is 'stunned' in her 'own dirt' having also experienced a stillbirth. The poem's conclusion has the mother tell us, as if the recipient of a miracle:

> Yet once it was done I got up,
> gathered my bedding
> and walked.

There are echoes here of the imperative ending of 'Irises / (Coda)', a poem in the sequence of 'Love-letter to Van Gogh': 'so what? Pick up your brush. / Get back to work'. If this section feels like an interruption in the collection, it is difficult not to read lines such as 'just ferry me through unharmed, uncut' ('Yellow Room at Arles'), and 'here, whatever sorrow waits for us, is hope' ('Pear Tree in Blossom'), without thinking of the poems that surround these poems.

The collection will go on to re-confirm love and to celebrate birth, ending with a magnificent antithesis to the cave-bear mother. Now the mother, attending her daughter, is:

> lit like this willowherb steeple
> disrobing itself in the sun,

> its long, unravelling hank of down
> wadded like cotton-wool
> its candelabra-d arms

> spent and beautiful. The breeze lifts
> and the meadow is flying
> with seed-threads.

> – 'ROSEBAY WILLOWHERB'

The world will once more be re-seeded. It is quite a journey to this bright point, but one that rewards the traveller.

Tom French's third collection, *Midnightstown*, underscores his place at the forefront of the Irish lyric tradition. If there is any justice, this work should find French given closer critical attention. The poems draw on standard lyric fare but they are beautifully fashioned and incorporate an aesthetic that engages with twenty-first century Ireland. Nike and Facebook sit comfortably alongside saints, sods and crows – the latter eating a discarded Chinese takeaway in a poem that has the symbolic ash seed germinating in a very contemporary Nike sole ('The Bridge of Peace'). That takeaway can trace its origins to Mahon's 'The Chinese Restaurant in Portrush', which signalled the search for new symbols for contemporary Irish poetry. And in 'Late Encounters', the ash seed can trace its etymological root to the surname 'French': 'To *French* through *de Freyne* from *Fraxinus*, / my father's name comes down to me from *ash.*' Both 'French' and French are enriched by the past but are equally engaged with the present.

This use of the ash seed is one small example of the subtle interconnectedness of poems across the collection. As occurs with Benson's 'Cave Bear', French's opening poem 'The Delivery Room' juxtaposes birth with death. The new father, rejoicing in the birth of his son, looks out of the hospital window to the neighbouring cemetery. In searingly intimate detail the collection will go on to expose the effect of a brother's suicide and, in a series of diary-like poems, to chart the progress of oncology

treatments. The honest and vivid evocation of suffering is all the more
potent for the delicacy of the execution. '02.07.2012' ends:

> On a morphine pump nestled
> between pillows, bearing beads
> of moisture on its breath –
> this is how kindness leaves the earth.

And after the son had read his brother's suicide note for his father ('Reading to My Father'):

> Neither of us knew what would happen next.
> A son reads to his father. The world ends.
> The son is driving. They are going nowhere.

If it can feel as if we are intruding on his grief, French also distances the
personal by employing extended conceits. 'In the Mirror' employs the
ritual of gentlemen's hairdressing as a metaphor for male relationships and
death. In part two, 'Thermopylae', Greek soldiers tie each other's hair
back so they might 'see the beautiful death they prayed to Eros for'. In
part three, French will trim his father's hair one last time, and we return
again to the implications and possibilities inherent in the word 'French':

> I present him with an eyebrow pencil with which
> he makes the F upright, its high rungs, the 'rench'.

Familial deaths are indeed a [w]rench, but *Midnightstown* is poetic
commemoration at the highest level. As perhaps French puts it best, in 'A
Water Trough in County Monaghan':

> When the bell's struck, its fresh note ripples.
> Striking the wrong note is unimaginable.

Gerald Dawe

EAST PIER

Not a bad day today
by all accounts. Little bits
of mist hang above
our encampments –

villas wedged into cliff face,
the grand terraces
overlooking the bay;
an older order of things.

Along with the sprightly
there's one or two giving
out on the latest iPhones
unassuageable complaint.

I keep to the east pier
under this cold blanket
of sky, patches of mist
like smoke from a fire.

Joe Lines

TEEMING DOWN

The winter afternoon has ebbed away by five.
Out past the range of the streetlights
the hills are massed like chickens asleep in a coop,
the mountain road is a tightrope.

The wind urges the car.
We drive under the door of the woods
and it's just the marine life of the dashboard lights.
There's something heavy in the rain,

more than leaves or debris, building
into a thick batting at the windows.
You drop down into second and then we see them stick
and smear on the windscreen their scales and bluish blood,

their fins not finding purchase anywhere,
dumbly bombarding the shocked acres of bracken.
I see a high tide pressing on the sunroof,
us capsized and cast away –

but then it lifts, leaving us on four wheels,
gaping through sodden hair.
The run-off thins the silver from the road.
By day, no fish in trees, the mountain as it was.

Siobhán Campbell

PERIWINKLES

Long after pollution was confirmed, you insisted
on picking periwinkles by the Bull Wall.
We swapped them in the kitchen for fresh ones
from Thomas's fish stall in Mary Street.
And when you went out door-to-door for Fianna Fáil,
they thought your northern accent helped to swell
the brand of softer nation they were selling.
Dev had been betrayed and those treaty chaps
were led astray, forgetting the sacrifice of the sixteen.
The inheritance was clear, a straight line right back
from there to here and a daughter who believed
not one word of it, until you took her up –
gave her the tether tour, backing around
Stranmillis to Malone. That's where Muldoon slipped
out a window of a night to meet his squeeze.
And there's the bay those giant roses set alight.

Jackie Gorman

PHOTOGRAPH OF WATER

The photo was taken the evening I drowned.
I am in the water just below the surface.
The lake is in a deep slumber
not woken by the pike
as it trembles through its dreams.
I can't say how old I am
as the water and light play tricks.
Look long enough and you will see me floating.

Maureen Boyle

AND YET WE MUST LIVE IN THESE TIMES

Sarah Clancy, *The Truth & Other Stories* (Salmon Press, 2014), €12.
Celeste Augé, *Skip Diving* (Salmon Press, 2014), €12.
Dave Lordan, *Lost Tribe of the Wicklow Mountains* (Salmon Press, 2014), €12.

Sarah Clancy's third book, *The Truth and Other Stories*, is playful ('ludic', to borrow one of Celeste Augé's words), deliberately mixing and messing with genre. The book's title, its cover and even its heft make it feel like a short story collection. It is full of shifting personas and voices that attempt to truth-tell in ways that are complex and multiple. The long prose poem at its heart, 'There's Only One Interchangeable Poem', tells intricate stories and then throws us by asking, 'if I said I was both parts of the dialogue, would that matter?'

Clancy may be Puck in her playfulness but she is also a poet of ideas; one preoccupation is with how to write in dark days such as these, days when poetry cannot be written, when reality renders metaphor redundant:

> they've built a fake refugee camp at Davos
> complete with soldiers and mock corpses
> so the rich can dirty their shoe soles
> can rough up their retinas in it
> and then call it experience

This is from an extraordinary poem called 'Selfie' in which Clancy wrests the word from its current meaning and invokes a weightier one, where, confronted with the dissonance of reality and spin,

> the self won't get up out of bed today
> and I can't say I blame it.

The very funny poem 'In Cill Rialaig Trying Not to Write "Digging"' deals with another day when poetry won't come, when the poet is sent from Listowel to a cliff 'for poeting', and, observing 'a big man / stooped over a turf stack', she prays that she will not go back to her cottage and write 'Digging'!

She wrestles with Heaney again in 'A Plague on all Our Houses', when she's in the region of 'Postscript' on the 'flaggy shore', but contests its famous injunction:

> that nothing has caught me off guard
> except how bitter these days are

[...]

> but I want to remember these times
> without metaphor

One of Clancy's responses to 'these times' is to write biting and inventive satire, as in 'Solutions to Homelessness', which offers a kind of Sweeney-like existence as an answer:

> Sure can't you live in the drainpipes?
> Or on one of those windowsills with the thin metal spikes on them
> if the pigeons can manage it, I don't see your problem
> are you a bird or a man?

This is an extraordinary collection in which Clancy's poetic voice ranges over political invective, lilting incantation, tender love poems and poems of empathy for the frail and hurt, and always with the recognition that, 'we are [all] hurt' ('And Yet We Must Live In These Times').

Celeste Augé's *Skip Diving*, her second collection, has a voice that is less peripatetic and seems to emerge from a more settled space than Clancy's, but it ponders many of the same questions, and grapples too with the question of how to write. 'Pace Notes' – based on the notes that rally drivers use to get them round a course – is a fantastic poem that negotiates the space between 'the house where I make poetry' – Annaghmakerrig – and 'the house where I live'. The psychic movement from one place to another is recounted as a kind of 'Wacky Races' – with Elizabeth Bishop her co-driver, Emily Dickinson her addressee, and St Brigit, 'the original Irish poet', her car.

Like Clancy, Augé too has days when she cannot write poetry – 'Today is Friday and I'm out of metaphors' – and the poem 'Friday' unravels in a moment-by-moment description of the day, until the second stanza reveals what has flattened it:

> Somewhere else a five-year-old boy picks up
> a fragment of a cluster bomb (where it might
> be windy, too) – they aren't metaphors
> either (neither the boy nor the bomb).

In 'Weekend Alone' the same imaginative empathy with someone on the other side of the world transforms the bleakness of a call-centre call into a moment of simple shared joy, '"It's raining here in Bangalore," / ... "it's raining here, too!"'

Augé's poetry constantly excavates, as in its wonderful title poem, the 'remnants' of strong preceding women in her life and of her younger self. The poetic voice often sounds surprised to find herself older and a mother.

In an astonishing sequence, she moves from this surprised self-revelation to poems dealing with female reproduction and the shameful treatment of mothers in Ireland's past, via audacious reworkings of the Leda myth. 'Leda Revised' opens with, 'There're worse things than being fucked by a swan' and looks at 'Sim-fizz-ee-otomy', while in 'Leda Does IVF', what enters her is 'a plastic speculum shaped like a swan's beak'. 'Aoibh's Baby Travels to Toronto (Without Her)' refers to the babies sent out from Ireland with only their names – 'hold tight, close your fist around your name'. And in a brilliant accompanying poem 'She Welcomes the World', Augé imagines the reverse journey of our age – the children of the poor in other parts of the world welcomed into Ireland:

> you are our brothers and sisters coming home,
> wrapped up tight in receiving blankets
> borne on the wings of scheduled flights.

Dave Lordan's *Lost Tribe of the Wicklow Mountains*, also a third collection, uses shape-shifting as a motif, and an epigraph from Vasari's *Lives of the Artists* relates this idea to formal variation. The title poem suggests this as a credo, the aspiration ...

> just to ascend
> With the lost and forgotten
>
> To summits the rooted
> Cannot even imagine.

In 'Discover Ireland' the second man in the abattoir's international line-up, the Estonian, 'sending money home / to see after the grandchild', whose gory job it is to slit the cow's throat, is transformed, by a kind of sympathetic magic, into 'Black-and-blue patches / reminiscent of cow-hide.' In 'Hope', the abstract word is transmuted into the demotic of the Dublin streets – a junkie or a drunk perhaps, diseased and dying, 'This time it ain't jus' a scare ya might really be dyin' [...] yer such a famished fuckin' wraith'.

The arc of this last poem is similar to the book itself, starting in desperation, descending into an apocalyptic Bosch-type landscape in 'Return of the Earl' and 'Spin' – which quotes Hannah Arendt, 'I am *the calm that has settled after all hope has died*' – but ending in a kind of uplift.

Many of Lordan's poems have the feel of parable or allegory, and at times I found it difficult to get past the – albeit brilliant – performative voice, with its repetitions of an opening pattern of language. But the book becomes more personal as it goes on, in poems like 'Notes for a Player', the very generous elegy to his father-in-law, Denis Boothman, and 'My Mother Speaks to Me of Suicide', a litany of the ways that young men are dying in Ireland, which ends with the assertion that they will continue to kill themselves:

> until this life, this incredible life I adore
> and which must not be wasted
> be made worth living and living
> and living again, for everyone.

The final poem, 'Love commands the neighbourhood', provides some sense of how this might be done in a powerful re-assertion of the message of the Gospel: an injunction to love the things and people that are hard to love, one possible answer to the question of contemporary living that all three collections pose.

Carolyn Claire Mitchell

SRUTHÁN NA LÁIRE BÁINE

Ní raibh mé riamh ann
ach cloisim é
ag siosarnach is ag slaparnach
tríd an talamh bán bánaithe –
na daoine óga ar an mbád bán
is seanduine le béal bán
ag labhairt le fear an raidió
faoi sruthán ag triomú
faoi láir gan searrach
faoi na fuaimeanna is na focla
ag imeacht bán
gan béala ná beola chun iad a rá.
Cloisim na focla sin ag stealladh uaidh
mar uisce geal ar thalamh spalptha.
Níl speach sa láir shéimh seo
í ina seasamh ar bhruach an tsrutháin.
Bíonn an seanduine ag éisteacht léi fós
agus tuigeann an talamh bán i gcónaí í.

Rody Gorman

from SWEENEY, AN INTERTONGUING

Sealgairí

Cé go bhfuilim gan cheol gan chodladh
Gan chairde, sin mé socair i gcónaí,
Sáil mar a bhfuil scol na lon
Agus bréagaireacht na sionnach
Agus crocaireacht na mbroc,
Dordán is búir na ndamh san eas thall
Ós aoibhne liom idir dhaimh i bhfeánna
Agus rith leis an damh rua
Thar an ré is leis na héin,
Guth chearc fhraoigh an tsléibhe,
Na ngearg agus na ngiúrann,
An rón ramhar, an míol má nach mall
Mar nach bhfuil fáil ar sheastán
Is gáir seilge na sochaí
Ó Shliabh Fuaidh go hÉadan Tairbh,
Léadaireacht na mac tíre
Is nuair a thagann geimhreadh donáil na gcon
Is na cúig cinn úd sa gcnoc
Is mé beo ar sheamsán is shamhadh
Oíche reo réaltanach.

Foragehunters

Although I don't get any songmusic or sleep and I don't have any respitefriends, that's me stillalways steadyquiet and heeltapeasycosy among the ouzelelks' call and the foxes cunninglieclicketlatrating and messbadgers' crockshriking, the homechampionox-stags' bassdronechant and lowbellowshouting in the erminewater-fall overby since I prefer to be bothbetweenamong homechampionox-stags in woods and run wtih the red homechampionox-stag across the moonageplain and with the birds, the censurevoice of the Jovemoormountainheathergrousechick, the quails and teredobarnacle-geese, the thick horse-hairseals and far-from-tardy plaininsecthares where there's no societycrowd standclamour or spleenquestprolehunting cry from the Fews to Edentariff, landsonwolves' rending and when winter comes the championhound-dogs' yelping and the mad Armagh bums in the hill as I quicklive on rivetdroneclover and sorrel on a starry hoarfrosty night.

Grá Dé

Seachnaím an slua.
Teithim romham roimh fhir is mhná.
Rithim le damh rua
Thar an ré
Agus ar an má
Gan anam beo gan Dia.

Tá mé cho sona liom ar fud na gcon alla
Ó Eachtaí go hEalla,
Beo ar chaora is ar chreamh
Is ar bhiolar mar bhia
Agus ar ghrá Dé
Idir thalamh is neamh.

For the Love of Charitygod

I shieldyieldshun the fairtarmycrowd. I shunflee from men and women.
I run with the red championox-stags across the mooneraplain and
on the mazeplainwithout a soul or God. I'm as happy on my tod
throughamong the wild championhounds from Aighty to Dulhallow,
quickliving on sheepberries and wild garlic and watercress for my lot
and charitygod love bothbetween earth and non-skyheaven.

Mioscais

Is fearr liom gan taisteal
Ach seo mé féin ar fáinneáil
Ó inbhear go hinbhear agus ó bhinn go binn
Agus ó ghleann go gleann ar fud Éireann.

Is mioscais liom daoine
Agus ní thabharfaidh mé taobh leo
Ach seo mé ag ochlán
Go bhfuil mé gan fear tuaithe gan chairde.

Is mioscais liom Dia le mo bheo,
Seo mé ag ceiliúradh is ag moladh
Agus ag guí rí na reann
Go bhfaighidh mé neamh faoi dheoidh.

Hate

I prefer not to have to hackletravel but here I am fannelfluttering from firth to firth and from horngableregardpeak to horngableregardpeak and from smoke-cloudhollowglen to smoke-cloudhollowglen amongstall-over the Irelandworld. I hate menpeople and wouldn't trustside with them but here I am whimpererlamenting that I have no countryman or respitefriends. I hate God all my quicklife, here I am warblefare-wellcelebrating and mollypraising and praying to the king of the stars till I get to the last non-skyheaven at last.

Cathal Póirtéir

LÁN DÓCHAIS IS GRÁ

Tadhg Mac Dhonnagáin, *Mise Raiftearaí: An Fíodóir Focal* (Futa Fata, 2015), €18.95.

This biography of the blind poet Antaine Ó Raiftearaí (1779-1835) has already scooped Gradam Uí Shúilleabháin 2015, the Irish language Book of the Year Award. Unusually, Tadhg Mac Dhonnagáin was doubly fortunate in being both writer and publisher, with his Connemara-based publishing house Futa Fata producing this handsome volume. (Gradam Uí Shúilleabháin has occasionally been criticised for prizing production values rather than literary merit in this award, but here the literary and production standards are both of high quality).

Mac Dhonnagáin paints a picture of a poet rooted in his own place and period that helps explain the extraordinary, long-lasting popularity of Raiftearaí's compositions. The book portrays a complex artist who expressed his passions in a range of verse: in political poetry, in works of praise for his native place, Cill Liadáin, in cutting satirical verses attacking those he felt had crossed him, and in love songs for several women he admired.

A great many people who have passed through the educational system of the Republic of Ireland will remember something of Raiftearaí, the blind itinerant poet of Connacht. Yet again this year I heard St Bridget's Day and the beginning of Spring referred to by someone recalling the lines learned in schooldays, and even the Taoiseach's announcement of a general election referenced a verse by Raiftearaí:

Anois, teacht an earraigh, beidh an lá 'dul chun síneadh,
'S tar éis na Féile Bríde ardóidh mé mo sheol
Ó chuir mé 'mo cheann é ní chónóidh mé choíche
Go seasfaidh mé thíos i lár Chontae Mhaigh Eo.

Many of us will also remember the artwork on the back of the old Irish five-pound note issued in 1994 in a series illustrated by Robert Ballagh, where the first verse of the poem 'Mise Raifteirí an File', is featured in Gaelic script on a classroom blackboard.

Many people probably have the image of a blind, itinerant poet and musician travelling the highways and byways of Galway and Mayo in the middle of the nineteenth century. *Mise Raiftearaí: An Fíodóir Focal* investigates the life story of Antaine Ó Raiftearaí and weaves a rich tapestry of history, lore and poetry that gives us a much more complete narrative of the poet and the time in which he lived.

Tadhg Mac Dhonnagáin knows as much as anyone about Raiftearaí and his long-term interest goes back to his Mayo childhood. His study of the poet's works and his life as a student teacher deepened his interest, and his work as a writer and broadcaster eventually spurred him to further research. He scripted an excellent television programme about the poet, broadcast on TG4 in 2010, and has continued his research since. The fruits of his labours are contained in this volume.

Printed biographical sources on Raifteararí are scarce and Mac Dhonnagáin has consulted works by Raifteararí enthusiasts including Ireland's first President, Dubhghlas de hÍde, Lady Augusta Gregory and, in more recent years, Dr Ciarán Ó Coigligh, the scholar responsible for the most complete and up to date edition of the poet's work. Their work includes sources from the oral tradition about the poet, as well as versions of his works passed on orally and in manuscript. The author digs further into that rich soil to unearth many new aspects of Raifteararí's personality, remembered in East Galway and Mayo for almost two hundred years.

Antaine Ó Raifteararí lived through an unsettled period of Irish history and his poetry reflects an active interest in the politics, religion, land and people that made up his world. During this time Daniel O'Connell became the uncrowned king of Catholic Ireland and eventually achieved Catholic Emancipation. While Raifteararí supported the 'Catholic rent' in his poem 'An Cíos Caitliceach', and praised the Liberator in 'Bua Uí Chonaill', this did not prevent him opposing his views and giving vocal support to the sectarian sentiments expressed in Pastorini's prophesies predicting the destruction of the Protestant Ascendancy in 1825. He also voiced his opposition to tithes and railed against Protestant proselytizers and Protestantism in general. The land question was another source of unrest and conflict, and secret agrarian societies were particularly active in Galway. The state's reaction to agrarian violence included executions and deportations, and Raifteararí composed a poem protesting the hanging of Ribbonman Anthony Daly for allegedly shooting at a landlord, while another composition, 'Bernain Risteard', protested the deportation of Barney Rochford and Pat Egan.

One of the achievements of Mac Dhonnagáin's treatment of the poet and his work is to deal with them in their fullest contexts, historically and geographically. He places him in the Gaelic poetic tradition, after the fall of the Gaelic order and the end of patronage by Gaelic chieftains. By the time of Raifteararí only part-time and impoverished poets remained, but the traditional power of the poet was still widely acknowledged and feared. This allowed Raifteararí to launch caustic verbal attacks on people with impunity until it led to the bitter row with the poet brothers, Peatsaí and Marcus Ó Callanáin.

Although reduced to poverty for most of his life, the poet was aware of the rich literary tradition that preceded him. Blind from an early age due to smallpox, Raiftearaí was nevertheless able to include references in his own work to poems such as 'Tuireamh na hÉireann' (1650) by Seán Ó Conaill, and 'An Síogaí Rómánach' (1650) by Cathaoir Buí Ó Maolmhuaidh. His four-hundred line verse history of Ireland 'Seanchas na Sceithe' displays further knowledge of the Gaelic manuscript tradition, with references to Seathrún Céitinn's prose classic *Foras Feasa ar Éirinn* (1634). Irish-language manuscripts containing poetry and prose would have been read aloud to groups of illiterate listeners anxious to hear the literature and history that had been handed down.

Mac Dhonnagáin places all of this in historical context by including potted histories of various aspects of Irish political, religious, social and linguistic history that played a part in the poet's story. While I initially thought some of this might be unnecessary, I found myself reminded of aspects I had almost forgotten and was introduced to others that I had never considered. I particularly enjoyed the inclusion of the folk beliefs and traditional rhymes that helped recreate the mentalité of the Irish-speaking Connacht of the time.

While his political poems open a window on rural life and Catholic sentiment during the period, it is his love poetry that has best survived in the living tradition. Fans of traditional singing will often hear versions of his poems in praise of Máire Ní Eidhin, Nancy Walsh, Brídín Bhéasaí and Máirín Staunton. Also sung regularly is his composition 'Anach Dhúin', about the drowning disaster on Lough Corrib in 1828 when thirty-one people were drowned as they were on their way to market in Galway, after their overcrowded and rotting boat was inadvertently holed by a sheep.

Another element of Raiftearaí's life that survives in the memory is the bitter and increasingly vicious verse feud between him and the brothers Peatsaí and Marcas Ó Callanáin. Mac Dhonnagáin structures this chapter to build slowly from initial jibes to an increasingly hurtful exchange of insults that culminated in the merciless public humiliation of Raiftearaí and his family. It is strong stuff, and gives us a fascinating insight into the place and power of poetry in that society. Ultimately, it is a heartbreakingly sad episode that left the poet a broken man.

The oral tradition that carried Raiftearaí's songs and poetry into the last century is paralleled by the high regard in which he was held in wealthier and literary circles in the years of the Celtic Revival. In 1900 Lady Gregory, William Butler Yeats, Jack B Yeats, Edward Martyn and Douglas Hyde were among the hundreds who attended the unveiling of a memorial stone to the poet. 'The satirical effusions of the famous Raftery' merited a reference in James Joyce's *Ulysses*, and John Huston made great efforts to make a Hollywood film about Raiftearaí, with Burl Ives.

Some readers will take a while to get used to Mac Dhonnagáin's corrective changes to the more commonly accepted spellings of the poet's name and places like Anach Cuan and Cill Aodáin, but the author explains his choices in the text. He mostly steers away from academic arguments but where they do occasionally appear they slow down the flow of the narrative somewhat. That said, it would be difficult to imagine such a full account of the poet and his legacy without reference to these.

This book is a celebration of the continuing appeal of Raiftearaí's poetry and his fascinating and tragic life. The blind poet's work offers important insights into the Ireland of his time from a perspective often ignored. *Mise Raiftearaí: An Fíodóir Focal* helps improve our understanding of the historical background and importance of that poetry which still lives on the lips of singers.

I will re-read the poems with added interest and understanding.

Aifric Mac Aodha

ANNE BONNY

I.

Mar go n-imíonn scáil
na deirge istoíche,
is an rud atá dorcha,
go ndéanann léas sa duibhe,
ní dubh atáid, a mbáid,
ach dearg, na hiascairí
mídhleathacha –

II.

Céard é an rud fírinne?
Stop, maith cailín –

An lá i ndiaidh na stoirme,
an ciúnas, an calm,

dhá thaobh an bháid
á cur faoi uisce, gan ghaoth,

sin rud a leathfadh anam.

Liam Ó Muirthile

RINCEOIR SPÁINNEACH
'Spanische Tänzerin', le Rainer Maria Rilke

Mar chipín solais sa láimh ag spréachadh i mbáine
sara bpléascann ina lasracha, ag preabadh
ina leadhbanna bíogtha – mar seo, fáiscthe i bhfáinne
teann lucht féachana, baineann sí tine chreasa a láine
as brothall damhsa teasaí, as a lár féin ag greadadh.

Agus ina laom lasrach i dtobainne, bladhmann.

In aon amharc amháin a folt gruaige adhnann
in éineacht agus le dalbacht cheanndána
ag fiodrince lena gúna iomlán sa dóiteán,
óna n-éiríonn, ar nós naithreacha geitithe, ciaptha,
a lomaghéaga eascartha, ag claiceáil, ag síneadh.

Ansin, mar a bheadh anam na bladhma spíonta
sciobann sí, caitheann uaithi í faoi na boinn
le gothaí an uabhair go tiarnúil
agus amharcann anuas: luíonn ansiúd ar lár, ar mire
ag preabarnach fós, ná ní thabharfaidh isteach.
Ach maíteach anois, le siúráil agus straois
chaoin an aitheantais ardaíonn sí a smig
agus satlaíonn á múchadh le buillí beaga na dtroigh.

Simon Ó Faoláin

LÉASLÍNTE
 – do Zoë

Bhí an *canary* chomh marbh le hArt le tamall,
Ach ar chuma éigin agus sinn ag glíomáil timpeall
Fé sceon sa dorchadas, d'aimsigh ár lámha roth an aerghlais
Is chas

Nuair a bhris ár gceann barr farraige bhí an t-ádh linn:
Cnó bán pleastach ar snámh i measc na raice,
Gur bhláthaigh – buí mar dhuilleog báite –
Ina rafta tarrthála

Brúchtann ollbholgáin aníos
Le cliseadh gach bulcaide.
Ná bac leis – ní hann dúinn san áit sin níos mó –
Ach tóg do cheann

Cé nach fada a mhairfidh ár stór bídh
Agus n'fheadar cén aimsir atá chughainn,
Nach álainn iad na tonnta seo,
An spéir?

Simon Ó Faoláin

HORIZONS
– for Zoë

The canary had been dead as a dodo this past while,
But somehow, as we groped around in terror in the darkness,
Our hands chanced upon the airlock's wheel
And turned it.

When our heads broke the surface luck was with us:
A white plastic nut swam among the wreckage
And bloomed – yellow like a water lily –
Into a life raft.

Huge bubbles belch from the depths
With the collapse of each bulkhead:
Pay it no mind – we are no longer in that place –
But raise your head.

Though our provisions will not last long
And who knows what weather front approaches,
Are these waves not beautiful,
This sky?

– Translation of 'Léaslínte' by the author

Caitríona Ní Chléirchín

THE PASSIONATE PAINTER

Gabriel Rosenstock, *Margadh na Míol in Valparaíso / The Flea Market in Valparaíso* (Cló Iar-Chonnacht, 2013), €15.
Gabriel Rosenstock, *Cuach Ó Aois eile ag Glaoch* (Coiscéim, 2014), €7.50.
Jack Kerouac, *sioc maidine / morning frost*, haiku translated by Gabriel Rosenstock (Arlen House, 2013), €20.

There is a certain search for calm, for stillness and for silence in Rosenstock's poetry. His latest collection *Cuach Ó Aois Eile ag Glaoch* bears witness to this lifetime quest for the essential silence at the very centre of existence and contained somewhere within language itself. There is a sense of déjà vu, of having been on a similar path before, an awareness of things fading away: the poem, the poet and the path. Here he distinguishes between 'ciúnas' [calmness, stillness , silence] and 'tost' [silence] in the following lines: 'is é an ciúnas a tháinig ormsa / is fada sa tóir orm é / ag glaoch orm as lár an tosta'. Silence searches for him, the poet and author of over one hundred and eighty books, the haikuist, the prolific translator, the essayist, novelist and playwright.

Cuach Ó Aois Eile ag Glaoch is one of his most beautiful collections, drawing together all the best elements of his work: his acute sensitivity and compassion with those who suffer, his mysticism, his ability to see beyond himself, to look outside himself, to look through things and through himself, such as in the dán 'Féileacán' ['Butterfly'], as well as his ability to see inside his own soul and into the soul of others. In 'An ghaoth ina tost' ['The silenced wind]', he tells us:

> Táimse rófhada ag féachaint orm féin.
> Nílimse istigh
>
> Is ní mise eisean an té sin amuigh.
>
> [I am too long looking into myself
> I am not inside
>
> Nor am I he that is outside].

Rosenstock's ghosts permeate this collection: 'géaga loma fuara idir mé is imlíne an duine sin / is mise ann // i m'fhinné taibhsiúil ar an saol' ['Cold bare branches between me and that outline which is me / a ghostly witness to the world']. Perhaps it is because he is so haunted himself as a poet that he is able to understand the ghosts of others and translate them, as in the case of his poem 'Góstaí Jack Kerouac' in this collection, and his exquisite translations of Kerouac's haiku and their (glistening) mist, frost, nightfall, morning and rain, in the collection *sioc maidine*.

In the morning frost	sioc maidine
the cat	coiscéim mhall
Steps slowly	an chait

No telegram today	níor tháinig sreangscéal inniu
– Only more	– tuilleadh duilleog
Leaves fall	ag titim

Frozen	reoite
In the birdbath,	sa bhfolcadán éan
A leaf	duilleog

Margadh na Míol in Valparaíso / The Flea Market in Valparaíso, his new and collected poems, gives us an outstanding insight into the immensity of his poetic achievement, by turns rhapsodic, innovative, sometimes gentle, sometimes ferocious. Some of his best works from the following collections are included: *Susanne sa seomra folctha, Tuirlingt, Méaram, Om, Nihil Obstat, Migmars, Rún na gCaisleán, Portrait of the artist as an abominable snowman, Oráistí, Ní mian léi an fhilíocht níos mó, Syójó, Eachtraí Krishnamurphy, Krishnamurphy ambaist, Tuairiscíonn Krishnamurphy ó Bhagdad, Géaga tré Thine, Bliain an Bhandé, Sasquatch.*

His empathy and understanding for the 'female condition' as well as the fact that the artist must distill 'sweetness / from the height of pain' ['D'fháiscis pian / as sárbhinneas / binneas / as sárphian'], even if that is the pain of rape, is apparent in his poem 'Billie Holiday'. Rosenstock is able to delve into the depths of the female psyche and the female experience of the body and in doing so he excels in the short-lined lyric. In 'Línte a scríobhadh le linn Chogadh na Murascaille, Eanáir 1991' ['Lines written during the Gulf War, January 1991'], we see how he is able to imagine, understand and empathise with the way women experience violent rape. Like his uncle Wolf, the lone cellist by the sea, who witnessed 'a woman / raped / twenty-five times / one after the other / during the Russian offensive'. The cello becomes metaphor for the silenced woman's body:

is ansin a thuigeas
a dháimh leis an dordveidhil
cois trá

foilmhe lomlán mhacallach na broinne
paitean cuar an adhmaid

it was then I understood
his empathy with the cello
   on the shore
the resonant hollowness of the womb
the curved sheen of the wood

Certain shadows pass through this work uncommented upon as yet, tragedies such as the 'first lesson in death; the teacher my father', in the poem 'In íoclann m'athar' ['My father's dispensary']; and although he opens his poems 'to bright things', 'somewhere in the world / a wall is falling on a cat / on a child' ['Osclaím mo dhán' / 'I open my poem'].

Rosenstock expresses longing, lamentation and loss with great delicacy in 'Liadhain':

Nuair a théann sí i bhfolach orm
chím gach áit í

Leanaim scáth an fhia
is an tseabhaic
líontar an doire lena héagmais

When she hides from me
I see her everywhere

I follow the deer's shadow
and the hawk's
her absence flits among the oaks

Also in 'Barróg scoir' ['Last embrace'] we get a feeling for the finality, the physicality and eternal continuation of grief. In 'Géanna na gealaí' ['Moon geese'], he refers to the cavity, the vast emptiness that the sound of the moon geese provoke in the heart of the Sasquatch: 'cuas ina chroí'.

Paddy Bushe's translations are powerful and vivid. There is an unforgettable quality to them, such as in 'Poema': 'Let slip the camouflage of your grief. Let your eyes / Focus on something besides the clay.' Also in 'Maenad' he captures the sensuality of the original:

In her womb she bears the constant sound of bees
That will be silenced only when a wave
Surges to her waist

She stands in the sea
Something unspeakable
In her almond-shaped eyes

'Meán oíche' ['Midnight'] is particularly strong as translation ...

Midnight in the heart of June
This great dark silence of birds
That cannot be known, only praised.
Out there in their thousands they are, beakshut,
Honeycombing

... as is 'Máthair' ['Mother']: 'Once he saw the scent / of his mother / lingering in milky light / / moon on ocean'. As Micheál Ó hAodha has commented: 'Rosenstock's poems have the stillness of paintings. They depict all the joy and sorrow that is this world of wonder'. The poet has a great feeling for colour, whether that be 'blue silences' or the rust on a German helmet in the flea market in Valparaíso. The 'world fades away', is 'an illusion', nothing lasts, but while it does, Rosenstock is all the time passionately painting on his canvas of poem and haiku, lest it shed tears of unlived life. He is 'the world's last dreamer', 'An t-aislingeach deirean-ach ar an saol'.

Patrick Cotter

OISÍN

With a dead tongue I named you
'little deer'. You had tossed under
your mother's skin, pushing shapes

like shrunken antlers behind a satin veil.
Somehow I saw it all leading to this:
the struggles with your mother

the scripted tears and slammed doors
the walkings-out and walkings-in
the candles lit and the prayers begun;

all to your father to be the first to hold you.
My green surgical gown, disposable
skullcap like some priestly garb

or butcher's apparel. You taking
the world in with a yawn, blood-stained
forehead and eyes blurred as if staring

through a dozen bottles thick with vodka.
The surgeon put a needle to your mother's belly.
Her trolley shin high in a swill of blood

and amniotic liquor. I cried God's name
silent, inside my skull. Chaffinch song
bickered through the open window like a chorus.

Gerard Fanning

LESSONS IN NAVAJO

It could have been that rich brogue I overheard
on the fire escape of a walk-up, looking out on the halogen-lit
pockmarked asphalt, half-built back parking lot,

of a midlands public house. And more hooch
than real contraband. But a stain lingers from the early
diamond white cold, where that late lost jarvey,

one over the eight, knelt to flush and flood pistons,
resorting at last to crank handles and those oaths you expect
from a man who knows too much, or just enough, of some

never written down Navajo. At some stage he wheeled
away in his buckled charabanc, as I, drifting from sleep,
salted half-remembered choicer cuts to practice in future

company, in that selfsame order of beer and bitters,
still and whiskey. Now it feels closer to the battlefield cipher
branching in the shipping lanes of the Pacific theatre,

where there was real purchase in a zigzag or stagger,
and the last of the Navajo nation swept a safe path home
spouting babble and baffle and sweet talk.

Gráinne Tobin

IT'S

It's the way the garden clouds over of a sudden,
an abrupt wind slaps at your legs,
rattles the petals off the roses.

It's drawers lying open in the kitchen,
exposing a rabble of lost things,
hard angles ready for bruises.

It's a smell of gas with no source
in present time – your hob's electric,
the swelling gasometers long dismantled.

It's the hush after switching off the landing light,
when the staircase takes a breath and holds it,
and your eyes open wide on the dark.

Ian Pople

THE DREAMS BENEATH THE SKULLS

Medbh McGuckian, *Blaris Moor* (The Gallery Press, 2015), €11.95.
Kate Newmann, *Grim* (Arlen House, 2015), €11.95.
Peter McDonald, *Herne the Hunter* (Carcanet Press, 2016), £9.99.

When Medbh McGuckian's 'The Flitting' won the 1979 'British' National
Poetry Competition, I'd swear an audible gasp went round the 'British'
poetry scene. Not only did 'The Flitting' seem so different from every
other prize-winning poem, but its difference was of a singular kind. Quite
quickly, 'The Flitting' was labelled *écriture feminine*. Elaine Showalter
defined such writing as 'the inscription of the feminine body and female
difference in language and text', and inscription seemed the essence of
'The Flitting', along with a unique sense of the domestic, the maternal
and an extraordinary indescribable power. And the poem, itself, has
become the subject of so much critical scrutiny that McGuckian might
feel somewhat hoist by its petard. But some of what that scrutiny meant
in practice is summed by the blurb on the back of McGuckian's new book
Blaris Moor: 'Hers is an art to be apprehended more than comprehended.'
So the reception to a new McGuckian book might be coloured by a particular set of expectations; a sense of the feminine and a need to suspend
disbelief and let the writing work its particular and mysterious magic.

    Blaris Moor does confound some of those expectations. An epigraph
from PW Joyce's *Old Irish Folk Music and Songs* of 1909 describes how the
execution, in 1797, of four young militiamen 'at a place called Blaris or
Blaris Moor', gave rise to 'a spirited ballad of eight verses'. McGuckian
then quotes Joyce's comment 'That the ballad should have been sung to
so many different airs and settings, in Munster as well as in Ulster, indi-
cates its widespread popularity.' Perhaps, McGuckian is simply allowing
herself the license to use historical source material in many, many ways.
And one of those ways is the group of four poems which begins with
'So Warsaw's Come to Wait on Us Now'. This group includes 'Notice',
which is almost an equivalent to Peter Porter's famous 'Your Attention
Please'; the poem purports to be a set of instructions for those 'People
selected for transport', and mimics language at its most plain and transac-
tional. This group of poems is most poignant in its direct address of war,
and McGuckian's ventriloquism of the voices of those people is assured
and moving.

    Elsewhere in the book there is more of the sinuous vivacity which has
been McGuckian's hallmark; though in this later work it is history that
seems to provide the parameters to that sinuousness, in poems such as

'The Statement of My Right Honourable Friend' and 'The Questioning of Soldier L'. In the centre of the volume is a sequence entitled 'Verses Unpublished in the Poet's Lifetime'; a sequence of five-line tanka-like vignettes. These short pieces are crammed with McGuckian's spinning out of imagery, as in 'Revenge against Music',

> He came from the depths of lyrical space,
> alias the summer on the one hand,
> to this mustering point, this profusion of lilac lustre,
> this home in the autumn borne along
> on its own words as though upon a raft.

Kate Newmann's *Grim* presents the reader with the dilemma that art depicting the Holocaust will always present: what is the relationship between the content and the production of the content, the art? The Holocaust is such an horrendous act in human history that judgement about it is only ever going to be of one kind. But art which takes the Holocaust as its subject matter, the art in which the Holocaust is represented, needs to be judged on its own terms, as art. There is art that does immediately reconcile these two things as, for example, in László Nemes's recent masterpiece *Son of Saul*. Kate Newmann's *Grim* presents much of the Holocaust in plain, unvarnished detail, as in 'Animal Vegetable Mineral':

> Families of Polish political prisoners
> could pay vast sums
> to buy back the ashes.
> It was very controversial.
> There was great doubt
> whose ashes they received.

Taking these lines out of the context of the book as a whole points up the difficulties of writing about the Holocaust. They have an immediate poignancy and testament, but are the lines poetry, or cut-up prose? And if they are the latter how do we understand them as poetry? Is their presentation of the content in this form, enough?

A number of the poems in the book suggest their provenance in newspaper reports. One such is 'Useless Eaters', which carries beneath the title, the following: '*Independent*, 5 and 27 January 2013', and many other poems carry such 'sourcing'. 'Useless Eaters' begins with 'Anyone with "disability" / physical or mental; / anyone with an illness / deemed hereditary.' The poem then goes on to outline the early measures taken 'against' such disabled people, then reports the development of 'vans / with sealed compartments / where carbon monoxide / could suffocate people in less than half an hour'. The poem finishes with,

> Walter Rauff,
> who designed the 'mobile gas chamber'
> lived, until 1985, in Santiago, Chile,
> no more regretful than any retired industrialist,
>
> drinking beer and dining on beef steaks,
> apricots, cherries, pisco sour.

Those final three lines are where Newmann's selectivity as the writer kicks in to elaborate on the original, unadorned narrative; and I rather wished there was a bit more of that. As in these lines from 'Thomas Blatt',

> Thomas Blatt never got used to the shock
> of white scalp
> as he shaved the women's heads,
> his fingers mute witness
> to the dreams beneath the skulls
> of those, *he* knew, were about to die.

These lines seem piercing and haunting in the way that their subject Blatt is haunted. And there are other moments in this convincing book where Newmann shows her considerable poetic powers.

Peter McDonald's *Herne the Hunter* is a very fluent book from a very fluent writer. It is the ninth book of poems from a writer in his early 50s, and who has recently published his *Collected Poems*, alongside critical works on Louis MacNeice, and other critical writing on Auden, Eliot and Hill. This book weighs in at some eighty pages, and is a very closely organised book. *Herne the Hunter* is split into two parts of eighteen poems each, and each poem is matched with another from the other half of the book, both in form and perhaps more glancingly in content, too. McDonald is a considerable formalist; sonnets, *octava rima*, villanelles, McDonald knocks them off with some aplomb. Each line is sonically weighty and usually very serious, and often the sentences run through the whole of a verse and both sentence and verse end with a resounding full stop.

McDonald moves easily from description to reflection, as in this from 'A Coach and Horses', a portrait of the driver Dulligan, 'A shape might come towards you, then be gone / nowhere, and there'd be only the leaves blowing / around upwards in front of you, and showing / nothing but the air they rode on'; McDonald is a man who sees clearly and who feels the natural world. And the best of the writing in this book has a palpability which fits with, and emerges from, the punchy language McDonald is good at. That reaches its apotheosis in the sonnets of the title sequence, in which McDonald the poet is a kind of tree-hugger. In sonnet 9 he writes,

> This last knock split it open, the maple wood
> solid until it's broken, only then
> coming apart slowly along the grain,
> not as strong as it's heavy, and though good
> for many things, not for this.
>   Whatever should
> have happened didn't: ten or a dozen men
> couldn't budge me, get me loose, or unpen
> me from the narrow cage in which I stood.

There's a slight problem, though, with the seventh and eighth lines, and the expansions required to fill out the form. Those of us who don't use rhyme and form so rigidly are often rightly envious of those who do. But there is also the suspicion that rhyme may give the writer a sense of where their next line is coming from, and that might be a substitute for pressure and urgency.

John Kelly

POEM FOR DAVID BOWIE

There was a man who used to cut the grass.
He used a scythe – the snaking shaft of it –
the sned – just right for swivel and for sweep.

A blade so sharp, they said,
it would cut wool floating down a stream.
And tonight I dreamed that man again.

Corrigan or Kerrigan – I forget his name –
but he cut a swathe. He cleared a path.
I saw the frogs, the twitching leveret,

the grasshoppers in splashes.
Then the sudden tilt in everything –
and everything collapses.

Bryce O'Tierney

STAR-CROSSED

Tonight the fog swept down the mountains and waits
at the windows.

There wasn't a horse fit to ride
at the shores of the Atlantic.

I look to the cooling bedspread
beneath my feet, his fist around the stone of a peach.

Claire Potter

A QUESTION OF TIME

There's a cup on my desk, someone's been here
before, in my chair, at my keyboard, it was this morning
when I tried to call you at home and got your mother
whom I was not expecting, so apologised saying
I had the wrong number. No, she said, who do you want,
You I said, but she replied, you were not at home. I felt
a nightmarish worry – I wished to cancel my subscription to
the waterfalls and the peaks and the lapis-winged dragonflies
to a heart that would crystallise into a long set
of principles, into harsh right angles, into the small
mouth of a pipe whose notes only played
but a summary of any true sound

Long days, tiny canoes of light
flitting across the grass once the sun goes down.
I want to wear black all the time to funerals
in my mind, I want to lie on a beach and fold
and bend and tear books into churches. As for the black
there have been poems and alphabets written about that colour –
Rimbaud's corset, his first heavy note, his sun gone down.
And whilst I might separate black from another colour
whilst I might stare into the garden, into the rain-streaked stones
and the damp wicker chairs seeing the grey of fallen
angels, I will wait too for the garden to end, for sunset to taper
– the wind whistling through an empty bodice,
the blue ghosts of dragonflies, principles, sounds
and a man and a compass sleeping in the same boat
unkempt and uncorresponding.

Notes on Contributors

Gabriella Attems was born in Paris and has lived in Austria, Spain, Sweden and Ireland. She is currently completing a Master's in Comparative Literature at the University of Vienna. Her translations of Charles Bernstein appeared in 2013 from Edition Korrespondenzen.

Richard Begbie writes in English and German. His poems have been highly commended in a number of Irish and British poetry competitions. His poem 'aal' was published in *Jahrbuch der Lyrik 2015* (Deutsche Verlags-Anstalt). He lives in Ittigen near Bern, Switzerland.

Maureen Boyle lives in Belfast. Her poems have been published in *The Honest Ulsterman, Fortnight, The Yellow Nib, Poetry Ireland Review, FourXFour, Poethead* and *Mslexia*. She is included in *The future always makes me so thirsty: New Poets from the North of Ireland*, just published by Blackstaff Press.

Marianne Burton's pamphlet *The Devil's Cut* (Smiths Knoll, 2007) was a Poetry Book Society Choice. Her collection *She Inserts The Key* (Seren Books) was shortlisted for the Forward Felix Dennis Prize for Best First Collection in 2013. Her forthcoming collection is on the life and works of Søren Kierkegaard.

Sarah Byrne (www.sarahbyrnewriter.com) was born in Cork and holds an M.Phil. in Criminology. She works in the field of restorative justice. She received First Prize in the Doolin Poetry Competition 2015, and was also awarded a Cork City Council bursary. She is currently studying for a Master's in Creative Writing at the University of Oxford. She has work forthcoming in *The Mays Anthology XXIV* and *The Fish Anthology 2016*.

Siobhán Campbell's third collection *Cross-Talk* has been reissued by Seren Books, and *That Other Island* is forthcoming in 2017. She has received awards in the National Poetry Competition (UK), in the Troubadour and Templar competitions, and was awarded the Oxford Brookes International Poetry Prize in 2016.

Michael Coady lives in his birthplace, Carrick-on-Suir, Co. Tipperary. A writer, photographer and sometime musician, he has published five books with The Gallery Press, most recently *Going By Water* and *Oven Lane and Other Poems*. He was elected to Aosdána in 1998.

Robert Colman is a writer and editor based in Newmarket, Ontario, Canada. He is the author of two full-length collections of poems – *The Delicate Line* (Exile Editions, 2008) and *Little Empires* (Quattro Books, 2012) – and a recent chapbook, *Factory* (Frog Hollow Press, 2015).

Evan Costigan has had poems published in *The Irish Times, The Moth, Cyphers* and elsewhere. He is a winner of the Boyle Poetry Competition and the Francis Ledwidge Poetry Award, and was shortlisted for a Hennessy Literary Award for poetry in 2014. He lives in Dublin.

Patrick Cotter has published a verse novella, two full collections and several chapbooks. New work has appeared or is forthcoming in *The Financial Times, Poetry, Poetry Review, PN Review* and elsewhere. 'Oisín' is his fourteenth poem to appear in *Poetry Ireland Review*.

Rachel Coventry lives in Galway. Her poetry has appeared in various journals, including *THE SHOp, Stony Thursday Book, Cyphers, Crannóg, Boyne Berries* and *Skylight 47*. She was selected for the 2014 Poetry Ireland Introductions Series and is currently writing a Ph.D. on Heidegger's poetics at NUIG.

Majella Cullinane, originally from Limerick, writes poetry and fiction. In 2014, she was awarded the Robert Burns Fellowship at the University of Otago, Dunedin. This year she started a Ph.D. in Creative Practice at the University's Centre for Irish and Scottish Studies. She was recently shortlisted for the 2016 Dundee International Book Prize.

Gerald Dawe has published nine collections of poetry, including *Selected Poems* (The Gallery Press, 2012) and *Mickey Finn's Air* (The Gallery Press, 2014). His other publications include *Of War & War's Alarms: Reflections on Modern Irish Writing* (Cork University Press, 2015). He teaches literature at Trinity College, Dublin.

Gerard Fanning has published with Dedalus Press since 1992. His awards include the Rooney Prize for Irish Literature, and literature bursaries from the Arts Council of Ireland. His selected poems, *Hombre*, appeared from Dedalus in 2011, and in 2013 a further selection was published in *The Wake Forest Series of Irish Poetry, Volume 3* (Wake Forest University Press).

Damien French was born in Co. Waterford and studied at University College Cork and Trinity College, Dublin. He is continuing his studies by distance at the School of English in the University of Nottingham. He lives and teaches in Japan.

Jackie Gorman is from Athlone, and was the winner of this year's Phizzfest Poetry Award. In 2015, she was a prizewinner in the Golden Pen Poetry Competition, and was also highly commended in the Goldsmith International Literary Festival Poetry Competition and in the Patrick Kavanagh Poetry Award.

Rody Gorman was born in Dublin and lives on the Isle of Skye. He has published poetry collections in English, Irish and Scottish Gaelic. *Chernilo*, his selected poems in Irish and Scottish Gaelic, was published by Coiscéim in 2006.

John Gosslee is an American poet, the editor of *Fjords Review*, and director of C&R Press.

Colin Graham is the author of *Northern Ireland: 30 Years of Photography* (Belfast Exposed Photography, 2013), *Deconstructing Ireland* (Edinburgh University Press, 2001) and *Ideologies of Epic* (Manchester University Press, 1998). He is co-editor of *The Irish Review* and curator of the Illuminations Gallery at Maynooth University, where he teaches English. His writing has also appeared in *THE SHOp*, *The Dublin Review*, *Edinburgh Review*, *Source* and *The Vacuum*.

Ian Harrow has an Irish-Scottish background. He was born in 1945 in Bamburgh, Northumberland. Formerly Head of Fine Art at University of Central Lancashire, his most recent of four collections is *Words Take Me* (Lapwing Publications, 2013).

John Hennessy is the author of *Coney Island Pilgrims* (Ashland Poetry Press, 2013) and *Bridge and Tunnel* (Turning Point Books, 2007), and his poems appear in *The Best American Poetry 2013*, *The Believer*, *Poetry*, *Harvard Review*, *New Republic*, *Huffington Post* and *The Yale Review*. Poetry editor of *The Common*, he teaches at University of Massachusetts Amherst.

Seán Hewitt was born in 1990 and read English at Girton College, Cambridge. His poetry has been published in *Poetry*, *The Poetry Review*, *PN Review* and elsewhere. He is a Ph.D. student at the Institute of Irish Studies, University of Liverpool.

John Kelly's novel *From Out of the City* (Dalkey Archive Press) was shortlisted for the Novel of the Year at the Bord Gáis Irish Book Awards in 2014. His poetry has appeared in various publications including *The Irish Press*, *The Irish Times* and *The Irish Review*.

John Kinsella's *Drowning in Wheat: Selected Poems* (2016) has just been published by Picador. He spends much time on the Mizen Peninsula, West Cork, and is a Fellow of Churchill College, University of Cambridge, and Professor of Literature and Sustainability at Curtin University, Western Australia.

Michael Lauchlan's poems have landed in many publications including *New England Review, Virginia Quarterly Review* and *North American Review*. His work has been included in anthologies from Wayne State University Press and Oxford University Press, and has been broadcast on *The Writer's Almanac* (http://writersalmanac.org). His most recent collection is *Trumbull Ave.* (Wayne State University Press, 2015).

Gwyneth Lewis was the inaugural National Poet of Wales 2005-6. An award-winning poet in both Welsh and English, she wrote the words on the front of the Wales Millennium Centre in Cardiff, where she lives. Her two memoirs are *Sunbathing in the Rain: A Cheerful Book about Depression* (2006) and *Two in a Boat* (2007), both from Harper Perennial.

Joe Lines lives in Belfast. His poems have appeared in journals such as *Causeway/Cabhsair* and *Cadaverine Magazine*, and have been published as part of 'The Lifeboat' series of readings. His work also appears in the anthology *Urban Myths and Legends: Poems About Transformations* (Emma Press, 2016).

Kirsten Lodge is the Humanities Program Coordinator and Associate Professor of Humanities and English at Midwestern State University. She has a Ph.D. in Russian and Czech Studies from Columbia University. She lived in the Czech Republic for seven years, and has published numerous translations of Russian and Czech literature, including Dostoevsky's *Notes from the Underground* (Broadview Press, 2014) and Karásek's *A Gothic Soul* (Twisted Spoon Press, 2015).

Seán Lysaght has published six volumes of poems, including *The Clare Island Survey* (1991), *The Mouth of a River* (2007) and *Carnival Masks* (2014), all from The Gallery Press. He has also published a translation of Goethe's *Venetian Epigrams* (The Gallery Press, 2008). His *Selected Poems* appeared in 2010. He lives in Westport.

Aifric Mac Aodha's first poetry collection, *Gabháil Syrinx* (The Taking of Syrinx), was published by An Sagart in 2010. She has placed work in various magazines and journals, including the Young Irish Poets issue of *Poetry*. She is the literary editor of *Comhar* and the Irish-language poetry editor of *gorse* and *The Stinging Fly*.

Afric McGlinchey's awards include a Hennessy Poetry Award and a Poets Meet Politics Prize. Her debut, *The Lucky Star of Hidden Things* (Salmon Poetry, 2012), was translated into Italian and published by L'Arcolaio. Her second collection, *Ghost of the Fisher Cat* (Salmon Poetry), was nominated for the 2016 Forward Prize (**www.africmcglinchey.com**).

Ben McGuire was born in Dublin and lives in Rome. His poems have appeared in *The Irish Times, Cyphers* and elsewhere.

David McLoghlin's first book is *Waiting for Saint Brendan and Other Poems* (Salmon Poetry, 2012). His second collection, *Santiago Sketches*, is forthcoming from Salmon in 2017. His pamphlet *Sign Tongue* won the 2014 Goodmorning Menagerie Chapbook-in-Translation Prize, and he was a prizewinning finalist in the 2015 Ballymaloe International Poetry Prize.

Paul Maddern was born in Bermuda and lives in Co. Down. *Kelpdings* (2009) and *The Beachcomber's Report* (2010) are published by Templar Poetry. He is on the Committee of the John Hewitt Society and has taught at the Seamus Heaney Centre for Poetry at Queen's University Belfast, at the University of Leeds and at Edinburgh University.

Martin Malone was born in Co. Durham and now lives in Scotland. He has published two poetry collections: *The Waiting Hillside* (Templar Poetry, 2011) and *Cur* (Shoestring Press, 2015). An Honorary Research Fellow in Creative Writing at Aberdeen University, he is currently studying for a Ph.D. in poetry at Sheffield University. He edits *The Interpreter's House* poetry journal.

Alice Miller is a New Zealand writer based in Germany. She is a current fellow at the Akademie Schloss Solitude in Stuttgart. A new collection of poems in English and German, *Blaue Stunde*, is forthcoming from Edition Solitude this year.

Carolyn Claire Mitchell is originally from Dublin and now lives in Co Mayo, where she designs and makes jewellery, writes and plays the button accordion. This is her first published poem.

Kim Moore's first collection *The Art of Falling* was published by Seren Books in 2015. Her pamphlet *If We Could Speak Like Wolves* (Smith/Door-stop Books) was a winner in the 2012 Poetry Business Pamphlet Competition and was shortlisted for a Michael Marks Award. She blogs at **http://kimmoorepoet.wordpress.com/**

Patrick Moran, from Tipperary, has published three collections of poetry: *The Stubble Fields* (Dedalus Press, 2001), *Green* (Salmon Poetry, 2008) and *Bearings* (Salmon Poetry, 2015). His poems have appeared widely in Irish outlets and also in the UK. He is included in *Windharp* (Penguin Ireland, 2015), an anthology of poems written by Irish poets since 1916.

Emma Neale is a New Zealand-based writer. Her novel *Fosterling* (Random House, 2010) was shortlisted for the youth category of the Sir Julius Vogel Award. Her collection *The Truth Garden* (Otago University Press, 2012) won the Kathleen Grattan Award for poetry. Her fifth collection, *Tender Machines* (Otago University Press, 2015), was longlisted in the Ockham New Zealand Book Awards 2016. Her new novel, *Billy Bird*, is due from Random House (New Zealand) in September.

Caitlin Newby was born in Los Angeles. She is currently a postgraduate student at the Seamus Heaney Centre for Poetry at Queen's University Belfast, and has had poems published in *Ambit*, *Oxford Poetry* and as part of 'The Lifeboat' series of readings.

Caitríona Ní Chléirchín's debut collection *Crithloinnir* (Coiscéim) won the Oireachtas Literary Award for New Writers in 2010, and her second collection *An Bhrídeach Sí* (Coiscéim, 2014) won the Michael Hartnett Poetry Award in 2015. She also writes reviews and academic articles, and is an Irish-language and literature lecturer at St Patrick's College, Drumcondra, DCU.

Štěpán Nosek has published two collections of poetry, *Negativ* (Host Publications, 2003) and *Na svobode* (Opus, 2011), and two books of translations, Conor O'Callaghan's *Seatown* (Opus, 2004, together with Tomáš Fürstenzeller), and Wallace Stevens's *Adagia* (Opus, 2008). He is a poetry editor with Opus Publishers. In 2002-3 he studied modern Irish literature as a postgraduate student at Trinity College, Dublin.

Sean O'Brien's eighth collection, *The Beautiful Librarians* (Picador, 2015) was a Poetry Book Society Choice and won the Roehampton Poetry Prize. His second novel, *Once Again Assembled Here*, was published by Picador in July 2016. He is Professor of Creative Writing at Newcastle University.

Edward O'Dwyer's poems have been published in journals throughout the world, including in *Poetry Ireland Review* and *The Forward Book of Poetry 2015* (Faber and Faber). He took part in Poetry Ireland's Introductions Series in 2010, and in 2011 was shortlisted for a Hennessy Award. He has been nominated for Forward and Pushcart prizes, and his collection *The Rain on Cruise's Street* was published by Salmon Poetry in 2014.

Rugadh **Simon Ó Faoláin** i mBaile Átha Cliath agus tógadh é in Iarthar Dhuibhneach. Tá trí chnuasach filíochta foilsithe aige go dtí seo. I measc na nduaiseanna a bhain sé tá Duais Glen Dimplex, Duais Strong, Duais Bhaitéir Uí Mhaicín, Duais Colm Cille agus Duais Fhoras na Gaeilge.

Nessa O'Mahony has published four volumes of poetry, the most recent being *Her Father's Daughter* (Salmon Poetry, 2014). She is presenter on The Attic Sessions (**www.theatticsessions.tv**), and teaches creative writing at the Open University.

Liam Ó Muirthile's next collections are *Dánta an Chamino de Santiago*, a trilingual collection in Irish, Spanish and English, and *Dánta Arthur Rimbaud*, including 'An Bád Meisce', a version in Irish of 'Le Bateau Ivre'.

Frank Ormsby's most recent collection is *Goat's Milk: New and Selected Poems* (Bloodaxe Books, 2015). He is co-editor, with Leontia Flynn, of *The Yellow Nib*.

Tracey O'Rourke lives and works in Palma de Mallorca. Her work has appeared in *Magma Poetry*, *Antiphon*, *The Montreal Prize 2013 Global Poetry Anthology*, *Ten Hallam Poets* and *Matter*.

Bryce O'Tierney holds an M.Phil. in Creative Writing with Distinction from Trinity College, Dublin and a B.A. in Violin Performance & Creative Writing from Northwestern University, Chicago. A performing violinist and poet from Anchorage, Alaska, Bryce pursues her interdisciplinary artistic practice through diverse contexts as collaborator, improviser, singer-songwriter and composer.

James Conor Patterson is 27 and from Newry. His work has appeared in *The Moth*, *New Statesman*, *Poetry Ireland Review* (Issue 114), and *The Stinging Fly*. He has read as part of the Poetry Ireland Introductions series and has been highly commended for the Patrick Kavanagh Award and the Bridport Prize.

Cathal Póirtéir is a broadcaster and writer. Among his publications are the books *The Great Irish Famine* (Mercier Press, 1995) *Glórtha ón Ghorta* (Coiscéim, 1996) and *Éigse an Aeir* (Coiscéim, 1998), and the audio CDs *Blasket Island Reflections* and *Traditional Tales of Wonder*. He is co-editor of *Iris IMRAM* and chair of Aontas na Scríbhneoirí Gaeilge.

Ian Pople's *Saving Spaces* (2011) is published by Arc Publications.

Claire Potter is from Perth, Western Australia. She has published a full-length collection *Swallow* (Five Islands Press, 2010), and two pamphlets, *N'ombre* (Vagabond Press, 2007) and *In Front of a Comma* (Poets Union, 2006). She lives in London.

Katherine Robinson holds an MFA from the Writing Seminars at Johns Hopkins University, and she lives and teaches in Baltimore. Her poetry, essays and fiction have appeared and are forthcoming in *The Kenyon Review, The Hudson Review, Ploughshares, Poet Lore* and *The Ted Hughes Society Journal*.

Gráinne Tobin, who lives in Newcastle, Co Down, has written *Banjaxed* (2001) and *The Nervous Flyer's Companion* (2010), both from Summer Palace Press. *When the Neva Rushes Backwards,* her English versions of Russian poems by Galina Gamper, was published by Lagan Press in 2014. She is currently seeking a publisher for a third collection.

Ryan Vine's work has appeared in *American Poetry Review, Ploughshares, Minneapolis Star Tribune, Verse Daily* and on US National Public Radio. His chapbook, *Distant Engines* (The Backwaters Press, 2006), won a Weldon Kees Award and spent time on the Poetry Foundation's contemporary bestseller list.

Jan Wagner is a distinguished German poet, essayist and translator. He has published six volumes of poetry, including *Regentonnenvariationen* (Hanser, 2014), for which he received the prestigious Leipzig Book Fair Prize in 2015. With translations by Iain Galbraith, a bilingual edition of selected poems was published as *Self-Portrait with a Swarm of Bees* (Arc Publications, 2015).

Grace Wilentz is a poet based in Dublin, Ireland. She earned her B.A. in English from Harvard, and is currently reading International Human Rights Law at Oxford. She has previously published poems in journals and magazines including *The American Poetry Journal* and *The Harvard Advocate*.